I Should Have
Stayed Home

I Should Have Stayed Home

The Worst Trips of Great Writers

Edited by
Roger Rapoport
& Marguerita Castanera

With a Special Introduction by
Mary Morris
and a Rebuttal by
Jan Morris

BOOK PASSAGE PRESS
a division of RDR Books
Berkeley, California

Book Passage Press
a division of RDR Books
P.O. Box 5212
Berkeley, California 94705

ISBN: 1-57143-014-8
Library of Congress Catalog Card Number: 94-70039

Cover Photograph: Wolfgang Kaehler
Cover Design: Bonnie Smetts
Book Design: Paula Morrison
Typesetting: Catherine Campaigne

The Publishers would like to recognize Wendy Ann Logsdon, Deborah Dunn, Elizabeth Kelly, Jan Yuen, Megan Quigley, Hazaiah Williams, Claire McKeown, Elizabeth Carney, Suzanne Simpson, Anuradha Desai, and the many others who made significant contributions to this book. To each of them we give thanks for a job well done.

Printed in Hong Kong by Twin Age Limited

To Oxfam America,
its supporters, volunteers, and partners across the world
whose hearts are in the right places at the right time.

Table of Contents

Introduction

by Mary Morris

RECENTLY I WAS asked to give a key-note address in San Francisco. I found the notion of a key-note daunting because for me the best that has happened, the most exciting and interesting, has always been the unplanned. I do better with improvisation. Like Indiana Jones, I prefer to make it up as I go along. This is why I am not a good person to send somewhere on assignment. It is like sending me to a party and telling me to fall in love.

If I hadn't been asked to give a key-note address, I probably would have just stood up and told stories, anecdotes of the strange and amazing things that have happened to me on the road. The time I found an Olympic-size swimming pool, filled with cool blue water in the middle of the Mexican desert, with nothing else there. And swam in it. The time when I lost my address book in Jerusalem and the quintessential tall, dark, and handsome stranger offered to lend me a hand, and I, a naive girl of nineteen traveling alone after the Six-Day War, followed.

But since this was to be a formal address, I thought I should write something down, whether I stuck to it or not. I called the talk—from which this essay is derived—ON TRAVEL AND TRAVEL WRITING: or Stupid Things I've Done, Horrible Places I've Slept. My basic premise was (and is) simple. Everything good that has ever happened to me or come my way has been unplanned. Everything interesting has been an accident. Misadventures can—and hopefully will—happen anywhere.

For example, the day after I delivered that key-note in San Francisco, I was waiting for a friend to pick me up at the Golden Gate Ferry Terminal. Somehow we missed each other. It was hot, I was tired, and my six-year-old daughter was restless. After waiting about half an hour, my daughter asked me for a quarter. I am a New Yorker and I know better than doing what I then did, but I was agitated because my friend hadn't arrived and my back ached. Judgment impaired, I rested my soft leather knapsack for a moment on the car in front of me in order to retrieve my coin purse.

Moments later a huge man with a beard accosted me. "Do you have any idea what you've done? Do you know what kind of person you are?" I apologized profusely for having touched his property (though it wasn't a particularly special car). But in trying to shield my daughter from this man's rage, I neglected to see the wife coming up on my side. "An eye for an eye," she cried, dumping her lemonade on me.

Whether we like it or not—and often we don't—mistakes, the serendipitous, the breakdown (automobile, not nervous) are the stuff of travel and travel writing. For me the most interesting things have occurred when the Trans-Siberian railroad made an unscheduled stop or when my bus never showed up at some crossroads in Honduras. My husband and I would probably not be married today if it hadn't been for the Navajo tribal police pulling us over for speeding (which we were not) and my brother forgetting to register his van—which we'd borrowed for a trip out West—within the continental United States.

Unfortunately travel literature—like all good literature— isn't born of comfort, but suffering. One fine anthology, entitled *Bad Trips,* is devoted to this notion. As Keath Fraser quotes Martha Gellhorn in the introduction, "The only aspect of our travel that is guaranteed to hold an audience is disaster.... That is what people like. They can hardly wait for us to finish before they launch into stories of their own suffering in foreign lands ...," but she is quick to add that "nothing is better for self-esteem than survival."

Travel writers, who are travelers first, are also survivors. And in reading and admiring the work of other travel writers, three things seem common to us all: an ability to find disasters, survive disasters, and learn about disasters.

Humor is the traveler's first line of defense. Travel without humor is like sex without love. You can do it, but what's the point, really? Whenever I meet anyone who is serious about taking a trip—that is, someone who has an itinerary and thinks he knows where he or she is going and what to expect—that is when I really have to laugh. Two of the funniest things I've ever read are when in *Shooting the Boh* Tracy Johnston's luggage is lost in Los Angeles and she has to go to Borneo, down the Boh River, without her air mattress. And when in *A Short Walk in the Hindu Kush* Eric Newby learns that his companion to the mountains of Nuristan has never climbed before.

I love things like that. I like to laugh at everything—native customs such as the Mexican propensity for posting a ferry schedule en route to Isla Mujeres (which bears no relation to when the ferries actually leave) or the way they look at you when you ask for a bathroom; the road signs which reveal so much about a place (again in Mexico, a woman's shapely body and the words "Curva Peligrosa," dangerous curves, in Vermont, "Lover's Lane. Road Closed," and in New Mexico—you may have to go and live in New Mexico for a year to appreciate this one—"Danger, Slow Down, Lake ahead.")

To digress back to the notion of digression, I am often happiest when I have no idea where I am going. A number of years ago I arrived in Guatemala City and went to the main bus terminal which is something out of Blade Runner — a surreal urban landscape of pollution, battered buses, and a seething mass of human life — and asked for a ticket to Salvador. And the ticket seller took one look at me and refused to sell me one.

"No," he said, "you don't want to go there. Go to Honduras. Here's a ticket to Copan." Copan.

"Sure," I said, "I'll go to Copan." I didn't even mind when he neglected to inform me of the overnight stop in Jocatan — a pit on the border (you get there too late for the border guards so you have to spend the night at the nearest town), a place where the hotel consisted of a straw mat on a dirt floor and the local restaurant strangled and plucked its chickens before your eyes.

I honestly don't remember a single Hilton Hotel I've ever stayed in, but I certainly remember that night on the straw mat in Jocatan while awaiting a pick-up truck that would take me at 5:00 A.M. into Honduras and I remember the fear of that chagras beetle that burrows into your skin and lays its eggs on your ribs and gives you a disease reminiscent of AIDS for which there is no cure. And I remember the hard plastic seats in the Jerusalem bus station and the scent of orange Fanta when the tall, handsome man in Jerusalem led me into the depths of the Arab quarter and then back to his dorm room. I refused to sleep in the cardboard box in Panajachel (you rent them for fifty cents a night), but I did stay in a tin box on my way to Isla Mujeres (a dollar a night). I remember the beds I fell out of in Russian hotels. And I remember the Old Mill Room at the Madonna Inn (I forced my family to stay in a different room every night, but my husband balked at the Cave Man) when our daughter turned on the mill at three in the morning, soaking us to the skin.

Where we sleep—not to mention if we sleep—are important memories for the traveler (perhaps more important than
whom we sleep with), but it is not the good nights sleeps we
remember beneath down covers in a cool room. Rather, it is
the night on the island of Viecques—a lovely place off the
coast of Puerto Rico that the Navy uses for target practice that
has a fine, grass roots resistance movement made up of local
fishermen and their battered boats—in a hotel under construction where the electricity had yet to be installed, nor the
mosquitoes sprayed (the natives had an idea of turning Viecques into a tourist attraction), where I flailed about for a few
hours, bristening the walls with the splattered blood of mosquitoes (my blood really) and then staggered down the road
to the nearest bar where I sang independence songs with the
locals until dawn.

And then there are the meals. No one has ever been able
to tell me with any accuracy what they ate in a four star restaurant in France five years ago, but I can assure you that the skin
of chicken's feet, dipped in sesame, and sea slugs on a June
night in China where a beggar woman ate off my plate are forever etched in my mind; and that I ate twenty-four cans of
sardines as I traveled through Russia, not because of Cher-
nobyl but because I could never find food. I can still taste the
paste of green tomatoes and almonds that Lupe made for me
on Christmas in Mexico fifteen years ago. And the pasta with
wild mushrooms and the bottle of Chianti Antonio the poet
ordered for me in a restaurant in some little hilltown as he
shouted his scorn of American capitalism and made me drink
grappa until 4:00 A.M.

But it is not our comforts we remember—or that anyone
else cares to remember for that matter. What is memorable is
misery. It is our dismay, our disbelief, and the fact that we

made it through. There is some perverse natural law which makes adversity lead to inspiration. I often wonder why I can't sit in a Paris café or in a nice Caribbean hotel and feel the travel writing muse. Somehow the lack of running water, the fear of disease, and the misery of a straw mat bring us closer to the brink and hence let us feel we are alive.

A night remains vivid in my mind—not one of particular risk, but of uncertainty. I'd met my friend, Carol, in Lima and we decided to fly to Puno to spend a few days before catching the Puno-Cuzco Express, one of the world's great train rides, through the Urubamba Valley to Machu Picchu. I had dreamed for years of Lake Titicaca and the altiplano, though I had not appreciated what it meant to fly from sea level to 14,000 feet (gradual ascent is recommended whenever possible).

En route to Puno we met Pippa, a British doctor, who wanted to go to the island of Taquille in the middle of Lake Titicaca. Despite the fact that I had a touch of the flu, we were game. So upon landing in Puno, we went to the lake. Driving along the altiplano to Puno the Andean people, descendants of the Incas who were herding their llamas and alpacas, waved. The reed boats on Lake Titicaca rocked in the waves while the snow-capped Andes across the lake shimmered. I was taken up in the world I had for so long wanted to visit and ignored the headache that had come over me.

The natives can tell you about *soroche.* In Tibet my guide kept shouting at me, "Morris, you have attitude sickness." Attitude or altitude, I was coming down with the high altitude equivalent of the bends. A migraine of unbelievable proportions for which oxygen, which was unavailable, is the only cure. But as we tossed our packs into the boat with the small motor that would carry us to Taquille, I was taken up by the beauty of the lake and its people.

of mind, to the way we have come to believe the world should be, but probably isn't.

Often I have wondered what has made me do these foolish things—go where I have gone, take the risks I have taken. (Though I must say here that before I had a child I would go anywhere and now I want the pilot to have his grandchildren's pictures on the dash.) But when I think about this urge in me to go places and take risks, I always return to childhood.

Somehow I cannot talk about travel and travel writing and not speak of my mother and the Suppressed Desire Ball. My mother always wanted to travel—London, Tokyo, Rome—and my father thought Oshkosh was far enough. His idea of a vacation was to rent a row boat on the Fox River and bring some take-out fried chicken along. But my mother had her sights set on other places, further things. She planned trips in her head the way I have planned them on maps. While her life was lived with Girl Scouts and barbecues and carpools, her dreams took her to far away places like Singapore, Dubrovnik, and Guanajunto.

When I was a child, my parents—this is Illinois, circa 1955—were invited to a Suppressed Desire Ball. You were to go as your secret wish, your heart's desire. My mother, who had a degree in fashion design from the Art Institute of Chicago, went into a kind of trance—and returned with blue taffeta, white fishnet. She had a dress maker's mannequin on which she began to pin the skirts. She went to a travel agent and returned with brochures. I'd see her downstairs late in the evening, cutting out the Eiffel Tower. "Mary," she'd say, "Where should the Taj Mahal go?"

Meanwhile, my father had no costume and my mother kept chiding him. "Sol, what are you going to wear to the ball?" The night of the ball, my parents appeared on the landing and

I, a young girl of seven, peered up at them. My mother wore blue skirts that flowed like the seas, her body was land, on her head a small globe turned. All the places she had asked me about were sewn into her skirts.

Instead of seeing the world, my mother had become it. Then I looked at my father and he looked handsome, ten years younger. That was because my bald father had borrowed a toupee from his barber and went as a man with hair. He won first prize.

When I was an adolescent I went with my mother to Europe for a summer and after that I began to travel. I traveled obsessively and I have always believed that if we know why we travel, why we write, or why we love what we love, we may stop doing it, so I just keep on and never question. In my early thirties, I went to Mexico where I traveled for more than a year and a half without much in the way of an address or itinerary. My father would write me letters which he'd Xerox and send to every embassy in Central America. I'd pick up the same letter in Tegucigalpa that I'd just read in Belize. A typical letter went like this. It included a clipping of a car wreck.

> *Dear Mary, this is your friend Linda's car, which went out of control and flipped over three times on the freeway. As you can see, the car was totaled, but miraculously Linda wasn't hurt because she was wearing her seatbelt. Hope you are taking care of yourself as well. Love, Dad.*

Somehow I have always managed to take good care of myself. It was quick thinking that got me to the Jerusalem bus station before I was raped, that convinced the Navajo tribal police not to arrest my Canadian companion—traveling without a visa and in a van they had reason to suspect was stolen, and made him ask me to marry him so he'd never have to face the authorities like that again. It made me tell myself that continuing to swim in the pool of the waterfall at Agua Azul was a bad idea and scream in horror as moments later a boy who was swimming with me went over the falls. It made me hide my journals as the Soviet border guards took me off a train.

I was glad I had my wits about me when I posed as a *New York Times* reporter at the Crystal Cathedral, covering their Christmas pageant, and they rigged me up and let me fly like an angel through the vault. I learned that I have a natural impulse to flap my wings. Survival is good for self-esteem. It is because of the unexpected that interesting things happen to us. And also because we allow them to happen. I know for me that it is because of the serendipitous, the sudden changes of plan, that I am alive. And I have lived to tell of it.

Sex and Coq au Vin

by Isabel Allende

I was conceived on a ship, in the middle of a storm somewhere in the Pacific Ocean, while my mother was seasick and my father had a toothache. Those circumstances determined my fate: I have been traveling most of my life. However, experience has not helped me to become a good tourist. I have no talent for trips, no sense of space or direction, no ear for foreign languages, and no luck with maps—it is hard for me to tell when they are upside down. Being lost is my natural state of mind. For some reason all the men in my life have been great travelers, starting with my stepfather who dragged me with him from one country to another on his diplomatic errands when I was a child.

In 1965 I was married to a man who had two passions and I was not one of them: chess and the Michelin guide. At the time people in Chile had a romantic idea about Europe—it was a sort of Mecca where one was supposed to go at least once in a lifetime to acquire culture and "see the world"—so we made plans to visit the Old World for a year to study and travel. Coming from Chile, at the south of the south of the planet, that was a major adventure. We will go camping, my husband decided, and I winced because we had camped the previous summer and we had been attacked by a cow, had found a scorpion in my sleeping bag, and every time we started setting up the tent, it rained. That didn't stop my husband, who argued that Europe is a civilized continent where rain is predictable and no stranded cows or inquisitive scorpions fraternize with people. So we packed our camping gear, an auto-chess game, and a pile of Michelin guides, and we sailed for Europe on a budget of one dollar a day. We traced colored lines and crosses on a map signaling the places that we wanted to visit. It was a rather ambitious itinerary, considering that we had no money and we carried along our two-year-old daughter, Paula, who was a stoic and patient child, but she hated traveling as much as I did. As soon as we landed in Belgium we bought an ancient Volkswagen that belonged to a hero of the Second World War. My first impression was that the car would never get us to all those places, but my husband explained that the Romans and the Crusaders had done it on foot and horseback and there was absolutely no reason why a German engine would not be able to do the same. In the following months I developed a strong antagonism against the Romans and the Crusaders. In Belgium we packed our bundles on top of the Volkswagen and set off to the North. The idea was to start in Sweden, cross the channel and visit the Brits, go all the way down to Greece and back to Belgium, for no other reason than it was in the center of the map.

For a year we survived on fried potatoes, horse meat, and instant coffee, while Paula's only nourishment was Coca-Cola and bananas. Things were pretty bad in the Scandinavian countries, where everything was more expensive and so awfully clean that we couldn't empty the baby's potty just any place, but they got much worse after the Netherlands. Europe on one dollar a day was a torture that is easy to imagine, so I will not linger with prosaic details about sadistic innkeepers, filthy bathrooms, and fleas. Paris was not hospitable, but baguettes improve greatly the taste of horse meat and with very little money we could enjoy the treasures of the museums at a student's rate, the beauty of the city, and the spectacle of the bo-

hemians in the Latin quarter. Looking for a nice camping place
we ended up in the Bois de Boulogne. On the calendar it was
already spring, but in real life it was freezing cold, so we were
practically the only brave ones in the campground, except for
a retired English couple with their dog, a hysterical poodle that
howled all night like a wolf, and a bunch of German tourists
in a couple of RVs who spent their time drinking beer and
smoking pot. Shivering in the frozen gusts of wind, we set up
our beat-up tent, fed the baby with yet another Coke, and
opened the map under the flickering light of a gas lamp.

France! Paris! My husband exclaimed with tears in his eyes.
We are in the very heart of the civilized world, the land of Louis
XIV and Napoleon, of Balzac and Sarah Bernhardt, of Sartre
and Brigitte Bardot.... While I opened a can of beans, I re-
minded him with a sigh that it was also the land of soupe à
l'oignon and coq au vin. I suppose that those magic words
triggered in his mind the memories of his mother's kitchen.
My mother-in-law was English—she could only cook boiled
beef—but she was such a charming lady that her meals were
considered exquisite by all of us. Love can play tricks. My husband looked at me with the twinkle in his eyes that I had seen
on very rare occasions, grabbed me in his arms with a passion
that he usually saved for chess games, and murmured in my
ear that I would have onion soup and chicken stew if that was
what I wanted. With a magnificent gesture he emptied his wal-
let, counted the bills, and announced that we were eating out.
A few moments later we were in the Volkswagen on our way
to an authentic French restaurant, the first in our young lives.

The park on a cold night is not as beautiful as it is on a
sunny morning: few cars, prostitutes, drug dealers, some young
people hanging around, police cars. We didn't know the city,
it was late, and we were tired, so we stopped at the first restau-

rant we found. It was a large white house in a turn-of-the-century style, way too elegant for us, but we were feeling rich, so what the heck. I think that it had an original name: Bois de Boulogne, or something similar. We parked, approached the building, and looked for the menu that is usually displayed at the door, but could not find it. We didn't dare go inside without knowing the prices. We peeped through the elegant windows at the people inside. Everybody seemed dressed in their Sunday-best; there were three old ladies playing a piano and two violins in a corner and we could see an army of waiters in tuxedoes moving in slow motion. Right behind the window glass was a table with two couples, a long white tablecloth, candles, roses, sparkling crystal, soft silver; the men had gray hair and silk ties, the women looked extremely Parisian. By then we realized that the place was well beyond our possibilities, but we could not leave. We were hypnotized by the atmosphere inside, the warm light, the faint music, and the relaxed happiness of the privileged customers enjoying the pleasures of gourmet food and a refined ambiance. Paula started crying and I gave her a piece of banana. At that moment four waiters approached the table, each one carrying a huge plate covered with a silver lid, and placed them gently in front of the patrons. They looked like dancers, their movements were perfectly coordinated. What was on those plates? Coq au vin maybe? I thought I was going to faint with desire. One of the waiters raised an eyebrow and at that signal all of them lifted the silver lids simultaneously, exposing the contents. Forsaken at the center of a big Limoge plate were three little shrimps, three miserable naked shrimps lost in the stark whiteness of that vast porcelain territory!

I couldn't believe it.... My husband looked at me and no words were necessary, we knew exactly what to do. We climbed back in the car, drove to a grocery store, bought a few cans, a bottle of red wine, and another banana for Paula, and went back to our tent. That was an unforgettable evening. We had a perfect French meal of soupe à l'oignon and coq au vin in the candlelight, not exactly within the limits of our one-dollar-a-day budget, but nothing extravagant either. That night I got pregnant a few yards away from the howling poodle, the German pot-smoking campers, and the prostitutes who offered their services in the Bois de Boulogne. I have always thought that, given the conditions in which he was begotten, my son, Nicolás, should be a loose cannon, but instead he is one of those straight guys you can always rely on.

The rest of the trip along and across Europe in that old Volkswagen was a disaster. As my belly increased in volume my soul decreased in hope; I really thought I was going to die of pregnancy. I developed an elegant technique of throwing up in public buildings and on freeways, and I learned to sleep on all fours because my back was killing me and I could not crawl into the sleeping bag or lie on the floor. I can't remember details of that long torment—in my memory all the museums, palaces, and cathedrals are a blurred mess, I don't know if I was in Venice or saw it on a postcard, if we stopped in the Côte d'Azur or in the Costa Brava, if we saw a bullfight or a horse race—and in the haste and confusion of exile years later I lost the photographs of the trip, so that part of my past may be just a dream. The only certainty I have is that I have never been able to eat onion soup or chicken stew again....

All the Way with LBJ

by Muriel Dobbin

THE LATE PRESIDENT Lyndon B. Johnson rarely missed a funeral, no matter how far he had to go. And where the President of the United States goes, the White House press corps, which has on occasion been mistaken for the cast of the Night of the Living Dead, follows.

Perhaps the most memorably awful of LBJ's travels was the time he went to the funeral of Australian Prime Minister Harold Holt, who had disappeared during a fishing trip around Christmas of 1967 and was presumed drowned. Many people believed he'd been eaten by a shark. Johnson decided he was going to Australia for the funeral.

The White House travel office swung into action with the efficiency for which it was known in those days. About a hundred reporters, photographers, and television technicians signed up, a plane was chartered for the press, and we were told that we all needed five shots, for everything from cholera to tetanus, before we left the next morning.

At the time, I was a White House correspondent for the *Baltimore Sun,* so I was in the line-up of reporters assembled in the White House press room to get three shots in one arm and two in the other. The President was there too; he appeared to be enjoying the sight of other people being stuck.

At 6:00 A.M. the next morning we were all at Andrews Air Force base. We boarded a Pan American stretch jet, the press charter that flies more or less in tandem with Air Force One. The idea is to keep in touch in case of a crash (of Air Force

One; nobody cares about the press).

The five shots began to take effect as the press embarked on what was supposed to be a forty-eight-hour trip to Australia and back. I was seated next to Frank Cormier, of the Associated Press, who was running a fever, and alternately requesting blankets and gin. This was before the days when reporters drank mineral water and communed chiefly with computers.

What we didn't know—I doubt that LBJ even knew, because he never made his mind up until the last minute—was that we were going around the world in about four days, most of it in the dark.

On the way to Australia, we stopped to refuel in Hawaii in the midst of a tropical downpour. Only the President and I were given umbrellas. He got one because of who he was and I got one because I was the only female reporter on the press plane. This was also in the days when the White House press corps was 98 percent male. By the time I got back on board, my drenched colleagues almost without exception had taken off their pants and wound blankets around themselves. The entire plane was draped with dripping trousers and smelled like a steam laundry.

Also on the way to Australia, we discovered that Dan Rather, then the CBS White House correspondent, liked to sleep under the seat. He negotiated with sitting occupants not to put their feet on his face then wrapped himself mummy-like in a blanket and stretched out below three rows of seats. It was unnerving until you got used to the idea, and what was most exasperating about it was that he would emerge without a hair out of place or a wrinkle on his shirt.

Canberra was notable for the fact that it was the only time in three and a half days that we slept in hotel beds. The rest of the time, we sprawled across each other in the plane as it whipped around the globe in the presidential wake.

The Holt funeral was the only planned event, and characteristically LBJ took the opportunity to stage a series of one-on-one meetings with prime ministers from Britain, New Zealand, and Singapore. He even got together with Harold Holt's grandson, and paid quite a lot of attention to Imelda Marcos, who was a very good looking woman in those days. We watched and noted and wrote and began to worry about the rumors that we wouldn't be home for Christmas.

The rumors proved to be true. The presidential entourage, trailed by the weary press, took off for what turned out to be Khorat Air Force Base in Thailand, where we discovered flying cockroaches and watched the President listen to pilots talk about the air war in Vietnam. It was then we had our first casualty. A photographer was carried off suffering from exhaustion and followed by several envious glances.

We soon learned that Vietnam was our next destination. A screen was put up at the back of the press plane so members of the press corps could receive hepatitis shots in its collective rear end. By dawn we arrived at the American base at Cam Ranh Bay.

LBJ was just hitting his stride. It had apparently occurred to him this trip was a good opportunity to traverse the globe. He also had a bedroom on Air Force One and was doing a good deal better than the press was. We had a full-time medic aboard by that time, ministering to high temperatures and swollen arms.

We never saw our bags after we left Australia because we didn't stop anywhere long enough for them to unpack the plane. This was the trip where I learned the value of a flight bag containing an extra sweater and underwear, not to mention cologne.

We never saw anything because we invariably touched down at night, and even filing stories was difficult. The usually efficient White House communications office had neither the time nor opportunity to set up a special telephone line or press centers. Instead, we had to use local telephones, which meant taking hours to send stories, and talking to editors who couldn't understand why we usually didn't know where we were going, or where we were. Newspaper offices in Washington, New York and London knew where we were, but we didn't.

We flew from Vietnam to Pakistan, where another photographer was carried off the plane on a stretcher, suffering from a heart attack. We were worried about him, but his absence meant there was another seat to sleep on.

From Pakistan, where LBJ had one of his double handshake-cum-arm locks with President Ayub Khan, we flew to Rome where the President of Italy and the Pope were waiting and Marine One, the presidential helicopter, tore up the Vatican lawn.

Rome was our last stop. We went home on Christmas Eve via Ireland where the press plane stopped at the Shannon Airport to refuel and also let the press do its Christmas shopping. The staff of the duty free store was waiting for us with open arms because they had been told Mr. Johnson was flying in. It wasn't until the disheveled, dirty press staggered in that they realized "Mr. Johnson" was Tom Johnson, a deputy press secretary who, years later, became president of CNN.

The White House gave each of us a photo album as a souvenir. It was full of glossy color shots of LBJ pumping hands and hugging people. It was billed as "First Presidential Around-the-World Trip." And it lived up to Johnson's campaign motto: "All the way with LBJ."

I had brought home some souvenirs as well. I still had bumps and bruises all over my body from groping up and down the aisle of the press plane and scrambling on and off press buses, not to mention all of those vaccination shots.

But I was grateful to LBJ. Within four days, I had dropped from a size ten to a size eight.

Into the *Denki Furo*

by Jeff Greenwald

MY GOD, IT was hot in Tokyo. The kind of heat and humidity that makes the jaw go slack. Morning was to stagger toward the newsstand, shielding my eyes from the glare off scooters and vending machines. Afternoons were spent careening through Tokyo in search of information, or prone dumbly on the *tatami* beneath an oscillating fan, listening to Tony Bennett on the Far East Network:

> *The little boy lost*
> *will find his way once more*
> *Just like before*
> *When lips were tender....*

Our apartment, like most in Tokyo, had no shower. But when the cool evening finally arrived I climbed gratefully into my *yukata* (robe) and made for the *sento* (public bath).

How I loved our neighborhood *sento*! Big bright locker-room-cum-gym, spotlessly clean. Please Leave Shoes At Door. Never crowded. A handful of Japanese men—I was the only foreigner—attended themselves naked and unselfconscious, rubbing their bodies with rough towels.

The walls were lined with low mini-showers. One must squat. Also, Please Turn Faucet On Slowly; those little Japanese showers can knock you across the room.

The entire back portion of the *sento* was occupied with baths. First there was an Olympic-sized hot-tub/Jacuzzi. Next to that was a cold bath, then a green bath, and at the end a small mystery bath, perpetually empty, with an alarming lightning bolt emblazoned in red on the white tile wall above.

Glancing now and again at that placid final bath, the surface of which seemed supernaturally calm, I felt a nagging curiosity. For all I knew it might have been a device for sterilizing surgical tools, or hyper-cleaning jewelry. Why was I seized by a crazy intuition to climb recklessly in?

～

There are no beggars and few elderly people on Tokyo streets. The city seems to belong to a youthful post-bomb generation that moves at ease among high, clean buildings and throbbing electrical billboards. As if there had been nothing before this. As if Tokyo had elected to submerge its history under canyons of steel and glass and especially plastic, infinite quantities of plastic. Flowers wrapped in plastic. Plastic eel in the windows.

Another day ended. I sweated and staggered from subway to subway, swooning in the unspeakable heat. Home at last and all I wanted was a bath. Collecting my toiletries in a plastic bucket, I set off for the *sento*.

There were men in the mystery bath.

Two old men, covered from neck to waist with outrageous tattoos. Their faces wore expressions of the purest transcendence, like samurai warriors under torture. One of them motioned to me with his head—a mere twitch really—in what seemed to be a gesture of invitation.

Silence prevails in the *sento*, but foreigners are expected to breach every custom and who was I to disappoint the Japanese? Pointing to the fateful pool, I inquired of the young man on my right.

"*Denki Furo*," he explained. Electric bath.

There is a moment we have all experienced, on the edge of

a diving board or at the threshold of a bedroom, when we know that to take another step is to commit ourselves irreversibly. I walked, naked, to the wall of the *denki furo*. The water within pulsed invisibly, and I felt the fascination and aversion one experiences when bending over to touch a completely still animal that may or may not be dead. But to touch the water hand-first would be, I imagined, shameful, as if I lacked the strength of my convictions.

Every eye in the room was upon me as I swung my leg into the bath. Electricity swarmed up my calf, buzzing and stinging. I uttered no cry. Bracing on rubber arms, I swung my other leg in. Face be damned; this was as far as I was going to go.

But wait—the bath was doing something, not unlike love, to my loins. They were turning to *soba* (noodle). Wearing the resigned grin of a fall guy in some '50s comedy, I began to sink gradually into the water.

There was no point trying to escape; my feet would not respond. The most important thing, I understood, was to remain unflinching as my testicles went under. Every situation in Japan is a test. I would not disgrace myself.

Contemplating the *wu* (essence) of the white tile wall I sank, expressionless, up to my neck. The men in the adjoining bath watched my eyes, staring with an impassive, cat-like gaze.

What did it feel like? Imagine the howling physical rush of a blow to the "funny bone," generalized over your entire body. Or think of yourself as a silver filling, and the *denki furo* as a mouth full of foil. Did it hurt? The exquisite intensity went far beyond pain. My only hope was that there would be no permanent physical damage; that, like the cartoon cat whose tail is thrust into a wall outlet, I would sizzle for a while then reappear, unscathed, in the next scene.

~

I do not recall how I left the *denki furo*. Perhaps the two old men lifted me, a recalcitrant tumor, from their buzzing province. Perhaps I mustered a supreme effort of will and climbed from the tub myself, like Batman in a fix. Or maybe I never left the bath at all. Perhaps I'm still in it, existing in a Borgesian dream-state of compressed time. It often seems that way.

I live in America now, where the burgers are charcoal-broiled. People take baths at home. I have never met anyone else who has taken an electric bath. We have all seen movies or read newspaper stories of people getting electrocuted when their radio or blow-dryer decides to take a bath with them, and I would go so far as to say that electrified water, like darkness or sharks, is a deeply rooted fear.

The men in the Japan National Tourist Board laughed when I asked them what I had encountered in Japan.

"*Denki furo*," they replied, unable to elaborate.

Still mystified, I called a shiatsu school specializing in oriental healing techniques.

"It obviously affects the polarity of your electrons profoundly," speculated the director. "It can probably alter your brain waves. After all, we're nothing but masses of electrons to begin with...."

Which explains some things. But sometimes, in Japan, there is no explanation save that single four-word mantra, uttered by the visitor in awe and italics:

They are the Japanese.

Night of the Army Ants

by Mary Mackey

MY SISTER AND I picked a good hotel: a clean place with white-washed walls, a quaintly thatched roof, toilets that worked, and hot water. It was a far cry from the other places we had stayed at during our two weeks in Guatemala. The room in Chichicastenango had been windowless, smelled of urine, had two straw-stuffed pads instead of beds, and sported a family toilet planted neatly in the middle of the courtyard. In Flores we had made do with a tin roof that leaked, chattering bats in the rafters, and spoiled pork for dinner. I had spent a good part of the past six years living in the jungles of Costa Rica and I prided myself on traveling tough, but my sister—who was new to the tropics—had had it. She had a stomachache (soon to become a case of amoebic dysentery that would ultimately land her in Intensive Care—but that's another story).

"For God's sake let's pay whatever it takes to get a toilet seat that doesn't fall off," she begged. She had been a great sport, but she was getting that glassy look in her eyes that meant she was about to crack. It was the same look she had given me when she was twelve, and I invited her to Mexico City, picked her up at the airport, and drove her through a riot, so I gave in.

That afternoon we checked into the nicest hotel in Tikal and spent the rest of the day in the park climbing the pyramids, watching the howler monkeys, and admiring the phosphorescent blue butterflies. At dusk, we even spotted a timid, deer-like agouti peering out of the brush. That night as we lay in our comfortable beds in our ever-so comfortable hotel, the jungle frogs sang us to sleep.

I woke in pitch blackness, some time around midnight with the distinct sensation that I was not alone. Suddenly, like galley slaves rowing to the same beat, a host of little things all bit me simultaneously. With a howl, I catapulted out of bed, and staggered around the room, slapping randomly. Roused out of a sound sleep, my sister went for the lights, but there were no lights. The electricity had been turned off at ten—not an uncommon occurrence in the tropics where fuel for generators is expensive.

"Help!" I yelled as I continued my St. Vitus dance around the dark room, slapping, stumbling, tripping over the luggage, and generally doing a great imitation of someone who had lost her mind. Being a level-headed sort, my sister located a flashlight, turned the beam on me, and to our mutual horror we discovered I was covered from head to toe with ants. Snatching off my nightgown, she began to beat me with a towel, smashing the little suckers, while I went on hopping and screaming.

When I was de-antified and a few degrees calmer, she directed the flashlight toward my bed. It was seething like an anthill that had been kicked in. Thousands of ants were crawling across the pillow and sheets, but that wasn't the worst of it: There were more ants streaming down the wall of the room in a column four or five feet wide and several inches thick. In many tropical buildings, the walls don't go all the way up to the ceiling. The ants had located the ventilation space and were rushing through it in unbelievable quantities.

"Looks like a goddamned waterfall," my sister observed as the slick, black column poured down the wall. "In a few seconds they would have gotten to my bed. Thanks for sounding the alarm. I can just imagine our skeletons lying there, picked to the bone."

Summoning what little dignity I had left, I brushed the smashed ants off my naked body.

"Army ants don't eat people," I announced. My voice grew shrill. "There is nothing to fear."

"How do we make them go away?"

"We can't. When the army ants march, the local people gather up all their food and move out of their houses until they've passed. The ants are a kind of pest control service. By the time they're done there's not a snake, rat, or bug left." I was always one for appreciating the balance of nature.

"Son of a bitch," my sister said. "You mean we're stuck with these things for the rest of the night?"

By now the other guests in the hotel were all awake, and, convinced we were being murdered, they had begun to pound on our door.

"Are you two okay?" a voice called.

We dressed, went out, and explained the ant situation to our fellow tourists. There were perhaps fifteen of us altogether, from Germany, France, Canada, and the United States, mostly young, mostly experienced travelers, but no one had been through an army ant invasion before. Since the entire staff of the hotel had mysteriously disappeared, we were on our own.

Sleep being out of the question, we arranged ourselves on the sofas in the lobby, pulled up our feet so the ants wouldn't crawl over them, and waited. A few people tried to make ant jokes, but no one was in the mood.

"I have to go to the bathroom," a German woman announced. Several of us picked our way to the door with her, but by now the bathroom floor was a heaving mass of ants. It was clear they were going to troop through every room in the hotel.

We waited. Above us, the thatch began to make soft rustling noises. Suddenly there was a plop, and a scorpion about the size of a human hand hit the floor running. Fifteen tourists screamed simultaneously. No, make that fourteen. There was one guy who wouldn't have screamed if you'd put a red hot poker to his forehead.

"Scorpions!"

"Are they poisonous?"

You bet they were. The old hands insisted that little ones were even more poisonous—even fatal—but that was small consolation. These were big, their bites could land you in the hospital, and by now they were falling like hail, dozens at a time, driven out of the thatched roof by the ants.

"Umbrellas!" a guy from Chicago suggested.

We rose like one person, fled back to our rooms, seized our umbrellas, opened them to keep off the scorpions, and retreated to the lobby, where we sat, hunched up against one another, like people waiting for a bus in a rainstorm. Occasionally a large scorpion would hit one of the umbrellas, bounce to the floor, and scuttle away, but it never got far before the ants mobbed it. After two hours of this, we were so tired we could hardly sit upright. It was then that a man whose name I never knew, but whom neither I nor my sister will ever forget, made one of the most generous offers one human being has ever made to another: "The ants haven't made it to my room yet. If you and your sister would like to try to get some sleep in my bed, I'll hold an umbrella over you." We checked him out. He was perhaps twenty-eight, thin, with dark brown hair, and he had a face that inspired confidence. Reassured that this wasn't some crazy plot to seduce both of us in the middle of an ant invasion, we agreed.

For the next few hours, my sister and I lay side by side in

his bed as he sat next to us, silently holding a large black umbrella over our bodies so we wouldn't get stung by falling scorpions. Somehow against all odds we fell asleep. When we woke the umbrella was neatly furled, and the chair was empty. He was gone, and so were the ants.

How I Became a Purveyor of Caviar and Champagne on the Trans-Siberian

by Alev Lytle Croutier

IN THE LATE sixties, Trans-Siberian had not yet become a sybaritic tourist extravaganza but served as a humble transportation vehicle that the Soviets graciously allowed other world citizens, who weren't fussy about their accommodations, to experience.

Carrying an English translation of Chairman Mao's "little red book," *The Thoughts of Chairman Mao,* which still was Chinese to me, I started my journey from Tokyo, my domicile for the past year, to the Cannes film festival, for the screening of a film I had worked on.

I imagined two weeks of gliding through expansive snow-covered plateaus, encountering larger than life figures resembling Omar Shariff and Geraldine Chaplin riding troikas in great furs, barbed-wired fences around torture camps from which no one returned, and a glimpse of the old Silk Road on which my ancestors had slowly trekked their way westward. I imagined myself disguised as a foreign correspondent or a great woman spy who would stumble upon some dark secret and become a pawn in a chain of impossible intrigues. After all, I was young and entitled to such fantasies.

My story begins at the port of Nakhodka, at the exchange counter. Utterly inept in dealing with money calculation, I had developed the habit of converting all my cash into the currency of the country I was entering—in this case around five hundred dollars worth of yen into rubles. And when I say all, I mean all.

We boarded the train in Khabarovsk and traveled through Siberia, vast stretches of verdant lands, mountains and plains, interspersed with colorless towns of lonely people who came everyday to wave at the train. Occasionally, we stopped to eat in those towns, a welcome opportunity since the train food tasted like dishwater. Our two "in-tourist" guides (synonym for KGB), named Andrei and Natasha, accompanied us everywhere.

Just as we were arriving at the last station before exiting the USSR, a voice came over the intercom. You must get rid of all your rubles before crossing the border. It is forbidden to take any Soviet currency abroad, Natasha translated.

At the exchange counter, I flashed my rubles and the record of the initial exchange at Nakhodka. The guy behind the counter shook his head and said, "Nyett."

"Nyett what? No yen. I don't care. In fact I'd prefer French francs."

"We can only give you back the currency you exchanged from and we do not have any yen here," he repeated.

"It's all right," I said. "I'll take anything, francs, dollars, pounds."

"We can only give you back the original currency."

"Then what am I supposed to do?"

He shrugged. "Either return them to us or you must spend it all here."

I inquired about returning to Moscow but my visa expired that very day and I had no choice but to leave the USSR immediately. I could not sneak out my rubles since I had already exposed them to the authorities; besides they would do me no good abroad, having zero value on the world money market.

The prospect of arriving penniless in Paris was devastating.

Where would I stay? What would I eat? I contemplated the railroad tracks, remembering Anna Karenina. My train comrades were sympathetic but helpless as I gazed at their consolatory faces.

Since I'd rather die than allow this bordertown bureaucracy the satisfaction of confiscating my last pennies without a decent return, I marched into the little gift shop full of the usual mementos one finds in border towns all over the world, even the communist world: lacquered boxes, fake icons, babushka dolls. (How many babushka dolls would I get for five hundred dollars?) Caspian caviar, champagne and vodka. That was it. I'd venture into my doom, plastered and debauched.

Suddenly, I had become a heroine in this tiny municipality. Crates of caviar, vodka, and champagne were delivered to my compartment by a retinue of happy sales clerks and porters.

Back on the train, I popped the cork and toasted my way into oblivion as we crossed past the agricultural fields of the Ukraine into Poland. Soon, a few of my fellow passengers joined to partake in my fatalistic endeavor. Others, looking for diversion, popped in, and offered to buy some of my champagne and caviar. Why not? I'd need a metro ticket in Paris. Drop the money in my tote bag.

As the days advanced, the motley stack of world currency grew, the spirits and the fish eggs diminished rapidly, and, under the influence, a great deal of intimacies were shared. Everyone on the train had become bosom buddies as the conductor announced, "Gare de Lyon." I splashed some water on my face to wake up and quickly gathered my belongings.

I handed the stash from my tote bag to the guy at the exchange—dollars, marks, pounds, liras. Obviously annoyed, he swore at me in French first, then handed me around seven hundred dollars worth of francs. I thought he'd miscalculated.

Not only had I retrieved my original amount but I showed a good profit. The pleasures of free enterprise.

I jumped into a cab and smiled all the way to my Left Bank hotel, amazed at the scheme of things. The "red book" was abandoned in the backseat for the next passenger.

A Winter's Night

by Eric Hansen

Note: After the shipwreck on Uqban Island (see *Motoring with Mohammed*) and the subsequent rescue by Eritrean goat smugglers, I returned to New York City on the night of March 3, 1978. The following story chronicles my first impressions of the United States after an absence of seven years.

Six days after leaving Yemen I was standing ankle deep in snow at the 42nd Street entrance to Grand Central Station. The time was 11:30 P.M., the temperature was around ten degrees, and I had twenty dollars in crumpled bills.

I hadn't visited New York City in seven years, and hope never again to arrive in the city under such circumstances. I had a sister who I thought might be living in New Haven, Connecticut, but her phone number was either unlisted or she had moved, and I hadn't heard from her in over a year. The first morning train to New Haven didn't leave until around 6:00 A.M. which meant I would have to spend the night in the hallways of Grand Central Station. The icy streets were brutally cold and I must have presented a strange sight with my deeply tanned skin, bright yellow foul weather jacket and pants, and rubber sandals with red wool socks. Most of my clothing had been abandoned on the beach of Uqban Island after our rescue by Eritrean goat smugglers, and I had bought the wool socks from a street vendor outside Victoria Station in London as a precaution against the New York winter.

Uncertain what to do to pass the time until dawn, I walked

to a Burger King where I nursed a cup of coffee for an hour and a half before being escorted to the door by a self-important looking assistant manager with a clip-on tie, acne, and dandruff. There was no point in arguing with the man. He was mindless, the coffee was undrinkable, and it was obvious I was there only for the warmth. I have since heard that the real pros can sit behind a seven-ounce cup of coffee for three hours, but as I staggered down the street, buffeted by winds that took my breath away, I realized that I was totally unprepared for a winter's night on the streets of New York City.

Back inside Grand Central Station, most of the regulars sat on inverted plastic milk crates or on the long wooden benches in the 42nd Street waiting room, but I had no desire to join these desperate looking people. A stranger, who appeared from the shadows, showed me how to stand on cardboard to keep the cold from coming up through my feet.

"The cold'll get ta yer bones and stiffen yer legs," the man warned me. "Ya can use newspaper, but corrugated cardboard's the best."

I took his advice and stood on two layers of cardboard. I also removed a folding knife from my pack and cut two foot-shaped pieces of cardboard that I placed between my socks and sandals. It made a total of four layers of cardboard and it seemed to help my feet stay warm. Barefoot zombies with blood-shot eyes, matted hair, and skin caked with street grime prowled the dark corners, and as a precaution, I put my knife in an easily reached jacket pocket.

I watched an elderly woman fall asleep on her feet. She was dressed in several long cotton dresses and a thin, blue nylon jacket stuffed with old newspapers and tied at the waist with coarse packaging twine. She leaned against the wall and locked her knee joints in such a way that she dozed off. Her head fell forward, but she somehow remained standing. I couldn't imagine the sort of exhaustion that would allow someone to sleep in such a position. I couldn't master the feat, and when I grew too tired to stand, I sat on my cardboard and quickly drifted into oblivion. I didn't sleep for long.

"Strike One" I heard a voice say. These words were followed by a loud tapping sound near my feet. I opened my eyes and a policeman came into focus slowly. He tapped the floor several more times with his nightstick while his partner stood cautiously to one side. Both policemen were properly bundled up in well insulated jackets, and equipped with service revolvers, handcuffs, and radios. Protruding from the cuffs of their blue wool pants I could see the tips of shiny black shoes.

"On your feet, my friend." The first policeman said.

"I'm waiting for a train," I explained. As I got to my feet the policeman took half a step back. *Could I look that bad?* I wondered.

"Let's see your ticket, buddy."

"I haven't bought it yet," I told him, before realizing how many times these men must hear the same reply each night.

"It's like baseball here," the policeman explained. "You get three strikes in this game. You can stand up and wait for your train, but there's no sleeping on the floor. If I catch you sitting or lying down you get another strike. Three strikes and yer outta here. The terminal is officially closed for cleaning at 1:30 A.M., but sometimes we bend the rules. It's too cold to put people out on the streets tonight, but if you can't stay on your feet you're makin' me look bad. Don't make me look bad. You've got one strike. Do ya understand?"

I understood.

The hall was filled with the echoing sounds of their heavy-soled shoes as the policemen walked past the old woman who was still sleeping on her feet. They had not spoken to me harshly, but the message was clear. For the next hour I remained awake by walking around the station. I had never taken the time to examine the vaulted ceiling that spanned the hall and, when I looked up, I noticed the ceiling was covered with the constellations of the zodiac. But even without this celestial touch, the strangeness of my situation, combined with my exhaustion and the behavior of the people around me, made it easy to imagine I was in outer space.

By 3:00 A.M. I could no longer stand. I knew I had to get some sleep, if only for twenty or thirty minutes. I pulled a piece of cardboard out of a trash can and looked for a place to curl up. I still had two strikes, but I quickly realized that all the warm, quiet, inconspicuous places on the lower level near the steam grates had already been taken by the regulars. I could feel warm air flowing from the maze of dimly lit passageways that led to the subway platforms, but I wasn't willing to enter the confusion of deserted tunnels at that hour. Instead, I found a urine-free corner and sat down with my arms around my legs. I placed my head on my knees and went to sleep.

I dreamed of the beach on Uqban Island where the sailboat had been washed ashore in a storm ... and of the peace and solitude of my two weeks camping on the island. Sounds of sea birds came back to me and waves lapped at the shoreline as I saw myself with a straw hat walking down an empty beach looking for turtle eggs. Shore birds picked their way through the damp sand and giant manta rays leapt into the air breaking the turquoise surface of our private lagoon. Then I heard a voice speaking to me.

"Got any inhalers?" the voice croaked.

I wasn't certain whether I was asleep or awake. I opened my eyes, but couldn't clear my vision. The last time I had slept in a bed was in Athens five days earlier. Dangerously exhausted, I stood up. My eyes burned with dryness, but the outline of a man became visible. He stood in front of me, just out of arm's reach. He was dressed in a T-shirt, two sports coats, and several pairs of bell-bottomed dress slacks. He also wore a neck tie neatly centered at his throat with a well-made Windsor knot. He didn't have socks, and on his feet were a pair of scuffed, leather shoes without laces. He was in his sixties and what I remember most about the man was the heavy layer of frost on his eyebrows and shoulders. Cold radiated from his clothing and I had the sensation of standing in front of an opened refrigerator.

"Inhalers?" I finally repeated.

"Yeah. . . . You got inhalers?"

"For what?"

"Inhalers . . . to stay awake!" He cried out in a crazed voice.

We stared at each other for perhaps ten seconds without speaking. I didn't understand what he was asking for, but I reached into my pocket and handed the man two dollars.

"Will two dollars buy you an inhaler?" I asked.

"Yeah . . . thanks," he said.

The man took the money and walked off. That left me with eighteen dollars. Years later I learned of a nasal decongestant that street people chew to stay awake when the temperature drops below freezing. The plastic containers are cracked open to reveal a cotton swab full of an amphetamine-type substance. One swab is approximately the same price as three cups of Burger King coffee, but it is guaranteed to keep you awake for a night. I don't know what these swabs do to a human body over the long term, but they solve the immediate problem of freezing to death.

In the cold I watched the clock through my steamy breath

and wandered about in a stupor. I couldn't imagine the effects of more than one sleepless night in such a place, or how the phantoms, who drifted around me, managed to survive an entire winter in these conditions. I heard a Tarzan yell from one of the floor grates, and then the echo of maniacal laughter followed by the hissing of steam pipes and a far off sound of someone pounding metal with a hammer. Then there was silence.

At 5:00 A.M. Grand Central opened to the public, but the first arrivals were the homeless. A small army of bag-people, who had slept elsewhere, trudged into the terminal to set up their territories for another day as the police moved about, quietly coaxing the all-nighters into upright positions. This was a scenario that would be repeated each morning of the cold season, until the weather improved and people could go back to sleeping in doorways or beneath freeway overpasses.

When the ticket kiosk opened I bought a ticket and made my way to the heated train where I sat, waiting for the journey to New Haven. The train began to move and I watched the landscape of a gray, northeast winter day become visible. A light snow began to fall and as the train moved north I found myself thinking about what I had seen the previous night, and what I had escaped. Shivering by the train window, with six dollars in my pocket and rubber sandals on my feet, I realized that there would be another life for me and, even then, I could see the humor in my situation. But I wondered about the others, the desperate night people moving through the chilly hallways of Grand Central Station trying to stay awake by chewing nasal inhalants and stuffing their clothes with old newspapers. It was a glimpse into my own culture and that glimpse will not go away.

Non-Stop to London

by Michael Dorris

In 1971, AT age twenty-five, I was set to embark on eight months of anthropological fieldwork in an Alaskan Athapaskan Indian village. The first question was how to get there from New Haven, and in keeping with the spirit of adventure, I decided to travel via London on Japan Airlines, which offered a stop-over. If I left JFK on Saturday night I could spend all day Sunday and Monday visiting my girlfriend Nancy, who had recently moved to England, and then on Monday I could proceed to Anchorage on the weekly non-stop.

The first sign that this was not the exotic international adventure I had hoped for came at the JAL check-in counter where a large sign enthusiastically WELCOMED a college tour of sheepskin-jacketed sophomores from Pennsylvania. Nevertheless, my seat pocket yielded, along with the traditional air-sickness bag and emergency card, dainty paper sandals, a "Happy Jacket," and a miniature fan. Dutifully, I robed myself like the airborne samurai I had intended to be, ignored the rendition of the Bucknell Fight Song which accompanied the firing of the engines, and awaited the hoped-for tea ceremony.

"Whereya from?" my seat mate demanded.

I thought of concocting a foreign accent and fabricating an answer like "Kathmandu" or "Vladivostok," but he barely paused for breath.

"Me, I'm from Staten Island, New York, myself. Unbelievable place. Ever hear of Tottenville High? No? Unbelievable football season."

And then he recounted it, every game, every play, every player, including frequent mention of Ricky Tantolino, his nephew, injured in the first scrimmage but gamely on the sidelines ever after. Sometime after homecoming, I began to cast furtive glances out the window for the White Cliffs of Dover. We were due to arrive in London at 8:50 A.M.

At 8:30, Tottenville had just been cheated out of the district championship when the airplane's loudspeaker erupted in an excited burst of Japanese. The heretofore implacable faces of the Japanese travelers suddenly became placable; as one, their jaws seemed to tighten and they unfastened their seat belts.

At last, an English translation was provided: "Your pilot, Mr. Ito, regrets to inform you that Heathrow is closed because of fog, so we will go instead to Paris."

Mr. Tottenville slapped his thigh. "Bad for you, good for me," he chortled. "I was going to Paris, anyway." Mysteriously, however, after an hour's flying time, no land appeared—just clouds.

Another two minute burst of high-pitched Japanese interrupted the Muzak. As the complexions of my Asian fellow-travelers paled to Noh hues, we were informed in English that, though Paris was, indeed, somewhere below us—and had been for the past twenty minutes of circling—it was currently experiencing a snowstorm and so was also closed to arriving flights. Captain Ito figured we'd better head for Rome.

Contrary to my forebodings, Leonardo da Vinci Airport was open. Following instructions, we debarked, boarded a small shuttle bus, and segregated ourselves into "Happy to be in Rome," "Wish we were in Paris," and "Wish we were in London" groups. Numbering a disgruntled twelve, the England contingent was the smallest but had the advantage of containing all nine Japanese passengers: two young student-types and seven businessmen. Besides myself, the rest of our little band consisted of a middle-aged Brit and a youngish American man. A Japan Airlines official with the improbable name of Gino Campanile gathered us together like conspirators. Heathrow was still closed, he informed we three English speakers, but JAL would like us to be their guests at a gala lunch.

With visions of Italian delicacies dancing in our heads, we followed him briskly to the airport dining room, only to be informed that there were no available tables. Our next stop was the cocktail bar where we were promised a drink and sandwich, but this room, too, was full. After much telephone consultation punctuated with shrugs and eyes to the ceiling Gino presented us with, as he called them, "the alternatives."

Plan "A" was that we should all board a Kuwait Airlines plane which was, at this very moment, preparing to take off non-stop to London.

"So Heathrow has opened," deduced Morris, the Englishman.

"Oh, no," replied Gino. "To our knowledge, it is still closed." Not pausing for objections, he continued with Plan "B": We would all go to a "seaside hotel," courtesy of JAL, and wait there until 8:00 A.M., at which time a JAL plane would "surely" deposit us in London, provided that Zurich, its first stop, was not closed.

"Will Zurich be closed, do you think?" asked Morris.

"I don't know, but I think so," replied Gino. He then asked us to make a decision immediately since Air Kuwait was awaiting our bidding, and he further asked that we reach a consensus, since JAL didn't want to be responsible for a "split group."

"But," sputtered Morris, who was getting upset, "if London is closed, how can Kuwait Airlines land there?"

"That, I do not know," allowed Gino.

Finally I asked Gino (with a wink to assure him that I was not as heated and demanding as Morris), what he would do in our position. He replied that since Kuwait Airlines was not known for their safety record and might well attempt to land in London, closed or not, he would "surely" opt for the seaside hotel.

The American (a doctor named Jim), Morris, and I, and the sole Japanese gentleman, Mr. Hiruma, who spoke enough English to follow the conversation, immediately voted to wait. Hiruma relayed the decision and its motivation to his co-nationals, and we all boarded a small airport transport bound, we assumed, for food and rest.

Instead, it pulled up to a Ceylon Airlines plane, bound non-stop for London. Gino, obviously relieved that his supervisory duties were at an end, proclaimed that London was now open and our luggage had been re-loaded. And so, we left the Eternal City, drank a cup of tea in the air ... and landed in Frankfurt. Heathrow was closed, it was announced in Tamil and English.

Grumbling, we marched into the Frankfurt Airport, but no sooner had we entered the building than we were out again, this time lured away by British European Airways. Heathrow was re-opening. Upon exiting the building, one of the Japanese students, looking frantic, grabbed me, demanding in a heavy accent, "Why are we leaving London?" There had not been any announcements in Japanese for a long time, and the depressed Hiruma had clammed up.

Flying time was to be an hour and a half, but in an hour and fifteen minutes we landed ... in Paris. London, you see, was closed.

Ours was a silent, dejected, exodus into Le Bourget. Through the frosty windows, we could see thousands of stranded people in waiting rooms, gazing longingly towards the Channel. We were given vouchers, but at the restaurant were told that the only food left was peanuts—of which we consumed large quantities. We waited, huddled on plastic seats or stretched out on the floor, until 11:00 P.M. when it was announced that London had closed for the night and we would all be put up in a hotel downtown. We were instructed to clear customs, find our luggage, and board a bus.

To no one's great surprise, really, our belongings were apparently headed for Colombo. Hiruma and I laughed rather hysterically. My duffel bag was stuffed with the carefully selected items I would need for an eight-month stay in rural Alaska, plus the written record of all my previous work there. His suitcase contained crucial papers for a business call he was scheduled to make from London the following morning. But Jim's situation was even worse: It seems he was a plastic surgeon, on his way to Newcastle to perform a series of cosmetic procedures. His trunk was full of plastic, which, if placed in too warm an area—like Ceylon—would melt.

After a forty-five minute ride through the snowy streets of Paris, we arrived at the Hotel Palais D'Orsay, a monumental relic at the Pont des Invalids which had been awarded, in 1948, four stars. There were already hundreds of exhausted travelers there before us, demanding suites with baths, and by the time our turn arrived, we were assigned tiny rooms on the top floor; fortunately we had no baggage to carry.

It was now 2:00 A.M., but I telephoned Nancy in London. She had called Japan Airlines continuously all day and had been advised by recorded messages (the first five minutes of which were in Japanese) that we were in, variously, Vienna, Dublin, Madrid, and Tokyo.

I finally dozed off, only to be awakened at 5:00 A.M. by a

French voice on the phone, and ordered "to make haste." With literally nothing to pack, I was downstairs in a flash ... only to be told at the desk by the giggling Hiruma that London had closed again and we weren't to leave the hotel for the airport until 10:00 A.M.

Our group of JAL veterans descended upon the ornate and unused dining room, where we were treated to a hearty breakfast of stale rolls and coffee, after which I improvised sign language to invite the Japanese student to go for a walk along the Seine. At every big building, he asked hopefully, "Notre Dame?" I'd shake my head and he'd look dejected. As we were heading back, he tried a last time, gesturing toward a small structure near the Louvre: "Notre Dame?" I figured he'd had enough disappointments in the past twenty-four hours, so I nodded my head enthusiastically, expecting a wide smile. Instead, he shrugged and said, I'm quite sure, "Big deal."

On the way to the airport, the bus picked up a few more British passengers who were quick to make analogies to Dunkirk. When we got there, surprise: London was closed, and we spent a foodless, chairless, seven hours browsing through the tax-free perfume display. Sad stories abounded among the displaced—there was, for instance, the weekend tour group from Lisbon who were booked for three days of London theater, dining, and sightseeing, but were now scheduled to go home.

And then there was the young actress I spoke to—very British and traveling with Mummy from Rome. She was to have had her "big break" today, she kept intoning, a TV commercial for chocolate Easter eggs, which would have been shown in Wales this year and hit Channel 1 in 1974—at which time she fully expected to be "discovered." Mummy, in an attempt to be positive, said, "Now, dear, just think of all those wretched sweets you would have had to eat."

45

Brigitte Bardot and her entourage were there, too, particularly plagued by a male passenger from a stranded Alitalia flight, who continuously slunk past her, eyes hooded but burning. Sporting her famous moue, Bardot looked through him, while the ex-Easter egg girl perched next to any man just long enough to hear him say, "*You're* far prettier."

Then, at 3:30 P.M., it was announced that the Rome/Frankfurt group (us) would be taken to a nearby restaurant for lunch. Ravenous, we assembled ... only to hear the further announcement that we were to board our flight immediately. As the engines roared and we taxied away from the terminal, we cheered and waved at the unfortunates within ... only to be told a moment later that the only airport in the United Kingdom currently receiving in-bound traffic was Edinburgh, so we would return to wait longer at Le Bourget. The Japanese passengers began to chant something that must have been the equivalent of "We shall not be moved." After some deliberation the captain announced that if it was Scotland we wanted, it was Scotland we would get! Morris calculated that we could at least take the ten-hour train ride to London.

And so, northwest we flew for nearly two bumpy hours ... and landed! ... but before the plane had come to the gate, Manchester, to the south, opened, and so we took off again and flew there. Just as we were preparing to descend, Birmingham, still closer to London, cleared and so we headed there, instead, and at last taxied to a full stop.

The airport was jammed with confused travelers. Just as I located directions to the London loading dock, a swell of Swedes inserted themselves between me and my non-English-speaking Japanese companions, and I watched in helpless fascination as they boarded a blue bus with the single word "Cardiff" above the windshield.

~

This story has a postscript. When Nancy greeted me at her flat with homemade tomato soup, a hot bath, and flannel sheets, I decided I was in love. I had already missed my connection to Anchorage and so, after a long sleep, Nancy and I had a blissful week together. On the flight across the pole, and then daily for two weeks from the Native village (with no telephones) where I was doing my fieldwork, I wrote her proclaiming my great affection ... to which I received no answer whatsoever. When her silence stretched to a month, then six weeks, the tone of my correspondence changed from peevish to hurt to outraged betrayal, culminating with a masterpiece in which I listed every fault I had ever found with her over the years we had gone out.

The very day after posting that letter, I received a fat packet of mail all bearing Nancy's London return address. I opened a note at random. The first line read, "I wish this damn postal strike would end."

Entering Paradise

by Judith Greber

BALI HAD BEEN a dream destination for a long time—my idea of paradise, with its beauty and unique, coherent, art-infused culture. Finally, in celebration of our thirtieth anniversary, my husband and I set out for what I fully expected would be the most romantic spot on earth.

We spent our last pre-Bali morning at Pramadan, a massive, ninth-century, Hindu monument in Java. Then with great excitement, it was on to paradise. Breezes. Beauty. Romance. Bali.

An hour before takeoff, we realized our passports and travelers' checks were missing. Undoubtedly, they were lying on an eleven-hundred-year-old Hindu staircase. As in gone.

Bali dropped back into the misty nowhere and neverland. We had traveled halfway around the world in order to become a dinner-party anecdote. "I know a couple whose entire so-called vacation was spent in an Indonesian civil servant's office.... Supposed to be a romantic escape, but of course, they got divorced at the end of it."

It's amazing how much attention you generate in a small foreign airport when you announce you've lost your passport. Words don't matter—the body language of sheer panic transcends communication barriers. My husband hyperventilated, gesticulated, and looked like a public service warning about high blood pressure. I became a mute handwringer, wondering what it would be like to live the rest of my life stuck in Java as a widow because my man was about to drop dead.

Then we had "The Miracle of the Outside Chance."

"What if," we whispered, "they aren't at Pramadan. What if they're in the car?" We'd known our guide only as "Eddie," not much to go on in a country of millions. But an undiscarded receipt shoved into the backpack had the tiny travel office's number on it. Garuda Airline employees formed a bilingual relay team and phoned the agency. Defying all odds, somebody was in the office and Eddie had not yet left with another tourist and ... and .... We waited, breath held until minutes before take-off when the driver roared up to the airport and Eddie, body half out the passenger-side window, swung our fanny-pack, passports inside, like a cowboy with a lasso. At long last, we were on our way to idyllic Bali. With luck like that—how could anything else go wrong?

Truth is, I didn't exactly feel like a traveler bound for paradise. I felt more like a piece of suet, with sticky clothing, runny makeup, frizzy hair, and a sweaty body. But I was sure all of that would change once we reached our hotel, the one the guidebooks called "lovely and authentic."

Our hotel was so authentic that it sat on the rice fields with its soaring thatched roof, its woven-grass half walls, and ... nothing. It was, in fact, a porch. Let us call it a sleeping pavilion. It was an extremely hot, open-air, sleeping pavilion with no fan to move the equatorial air, and no mosquito netting. And we had paid for a long stay in advance.

My husband looked a lot like a martyred saint—a sweating saint with a fanny pack stapled to his flesh—a sweating saint whose wife was the one who'd wanted this trip.

We were too exhausted and hot to walk the mile or so into town. For a fee, the hotel provided a car and a child barely out of diapers who viewed our presence as his chance to learn to drive. It was amazing how many dips and lurches the creative boy crammed into such a short distance.

By then, I was into serious meltdown, nauseated, and dreading the ride back.

Once back, my husband staggered into the porch, closed his eyes—probably in avoidance—and was out.

Ah, the fabled romance of it all.

I sprayed my entire body with eau de insect repellent and climbed into bed. I refused to be troubled by the room's other tenants—the lizard curled around the dim bedside lamp, the critters croaking in annoyance above my head, the jungle symphony of shrieks, grunts, barks, moos, gribbits, and warbles, and the whisk of wings inside and outside our room. (F.Y.I.: roosters crow at daybreak, but also at midnight, 3:00 A.M., 3:15 A.M., and whenever else the mood strikes them. At least they do in Bali.)

At dawn, my husband's voice floated over to me.

"Fourteen separate species woke me up last night," he said. "I counted." But he sounded more bemused than bothered by the zoological disruptions, and once again, I became hopeful.

And then he sat up, looked at me and said, with a sudden burst of animation, "Yuck!"

Yuck? In Bali? On this celebration of our years together? *Yuck?*

'Yuck' was *le mot juste*. The illiterate insects hadn't read the label. I had sprayed with repellent, but nonetheless I had been the object of obsessive buggy affection. Talk about fatal attractions—these guys were, quite literally, stuck on me.

My entire body was littered with their wings and heads and antennae. And did you know that repellent also melts nail polish, enabling pest-parts to fuzz even the fingertips?

At this point, what could we do except laugh? Which is not a bad, working definition of true romance.

That was when the real vacation began.

The bugs turned out to be a one night stand. We found better drivers and it cooled down. As for Bali, in every way it proved the equal of my fantasies. Beautiful, joyous—and yes, romantic—Bali shimmers in my memory as pure magic.

I should have remembered that all real magic requires a rite of passage, an initiation.

Enlightened Sahib

by Dominique Lapierre

IN FIFTY YEARS of constant wanderings on the roads of the world, I thought I had been through all possible—or rather impossible—situations. Until I reached a slum in Calcutta with the paradoxical name: City of Joy. Imagine an urban village where some 75,000 people are crammed on the space of about two football fields. It is the highest human concentration on earth. With only one water fountain and one latrine for 2,500 inhabitants. And yet, in this place which looked to me like hell on earth, I was to find more heroism, more love, more sharing, and ultimately more happiness than in many a city of the affluent West. Being there would change my life forever.

It all began with a night which will always be imprinted in my memory as the worst travel experience I ever went through. Why did I ever accept Stefan Kovalski's hospitality in that wretched place called the "City of Joy"? Kovalski was a Catholic priest who had come from his native Poland to share the life of the poorest of the poor in the slums of Calcutta. His room was a windowless hovel scarcely more than one yard wide and twice as long. The floor was of beaten earth and through the missing tiles of the roof, one could see pieces of the sky. There was no furniture, no electricity, no running water. Along the two planks nailed together which served as a door, ran an open drain overflowing with black slime. Kovalski considered himself privileged. He had the room all for himself, when ten or twelve persons were usually living in huts like this.

Before we retired in our hovel, Kovalski decided to take me

I'm sure I would have been fine if it hadn't been for the storm. It came out of nowhere. Black clouds, high seas, driving rain. Pippa turned to me after a while where I lay drenched and tossing at the bottom of the boat, and thought that I was making medical history. She knew of no cases of simultaneous intense altitude and sea sickness and thought she might write me up.

Our boat pilot pulled his craft into a shelter of reeds where we waited out the storm. It was dark when we set off again and through my headache and nausea I was only vaguely concerned about where the island lay. It was indeed ahead of us but we didn't know that we would have to scale a small mountain in the dark with our packs to get to where we might eat and lodge. Bidding our boatmen good-bye, we scaled the hills until we reached a path. Following the path we came to what appeared to be a small cave with a light coming from the inside, and a curtain across the steep entry.

I pulled back the curtain and saw inside four men in wide-rimmed black hats and black capes, smoking cigarettes and playing cards on a stone slab, and a woman stirring a cauldron that was heating over a fire. She tossed something from the cauldron onto tin plates and bid us to sit down. The men glanced up from their card game and made room for us on the slab. We ate what was on the plates—which I prefer to believe was mutton stew—and were shown to a hut on stilts. I cannot discuss the sanitary conditions because there were none.

The most interesting things I have seen and the strange things that have happened to me all occurred because I was lost or wandered off, there was no room at the inn or the bus broke down. For the traveler and travel writer digression can and should be a way of life. There must be some risk involved, if not to life and limb, at least to psyche, to complacent state out for dinner. It was an occasion to discover that even in the depths of hell one could write a Michelin guide; there were all sorts of small restaurants in the alleys of the City of Joy. Their food went from the most abject refuse to four star gastronomy, by slum standards, of course. Kovalski chose his favorite place. He referred to it as "the Maxim's of the neighborhood." It belonged to a fat, bald headed Muslim called Nasser, who presided over his steaming caldron like a Buddha behind an incense burner. We sat at a table. A fan, apparently on the point of expiring, was stirring up a torrid atmosphere, heavy with the smell of frying. The specialty of the establishment was "buffalo stew." My companion smiled at the surprise I showed when one of the young serving boys put in front of me a plate filled with this strange delicacy.

"It's not real stew," he said, mopping greedily at his plate. "Just the sauce. There isn't any meat in it. But the bones, skin, marrow and gelatin of the buffalo have been so well simmered that it's full of proteins. It's just like eating a New York sirloin!"

On our way home we drank tea from the tea-stall of Surya, the Hindu holy man living across from Kovalski. It was a heavy mixture of tea, milk and sugar served in a tiny terra-cotta cup which you broke afterwards.

It was already dark when we reached our hovel. Night falls very early in the tropics. My presence seemed to trigger an intense curiosity from the neighbors. Who was that crazy Sahib who had come to share the sleep of the poor? Kovalski lit an oil lamp and we laid down on the barren floor. In the vacillating light which drew shadows on the wall, I discovered one photograph pinned up on the wall. It was the image of the Sacred Shroud of Turin, the face of Christ imprinted on his shroud, an opportune presence in the midst of the suffering humanity surrounding us. Towards 9:00 P.M., as the noise of the alleys died away, I became aware of the echoes of the life around me: conversations in the nearby hovels, arguments, tears, fits of coughing. Sometimes the coughing was so loud that it seemed everyone in the slum suffered from pulmonary disease. Numb with fatigue and emotion, I folded my shirt and jeans to form a pillow and stretched out on the small straw mat Kovalski had unrolled for me. Then my companion blew out the oil lamp.

It was then that a frenzied chorus struck up right above our heads. Kovalski struck a match and I discovered a team of rats chasing one another about on the bamboo framing, rushing down the walls in a cacophony of shrill cries. Terrified, I leapt to my feet and, a shoe in each hand, threatened the intruders. But as fast as one group made off, others arrived through the holes of the roof. Apparently undisturbed, Kovalski watched my efforts with an air of indulgence. He must have felt I had a long way to go before attaining the nonviolent serenity of my idol Mahatma Gandhi. The magnitude of the invasion finally forced me to give up. With resignation, I laid down again, but almost immediately I felt something stirring in my hair. I struck a match, and shaking my head I saw an enormous hairy centipede fall out of it. Kovalski informed me that the creature was a scolopendra whose sting could be as venomous as a scorpion's.

At this point I was furiously tempted to dress and run to the closest taxi stand and have myself driven to the nearest Hilton. But I decided to give my experience in a slum one more chance. How right I was. The City of Joy had further surprises in store for me. No sooner had darkness enveloped our hovel once again when I heard a strange rattling. I begged Kovalski to light his lamp. There were battalions of cockroaches coming down from the roof. Hundreds, thousands of them. Suddenly I saw an incredible spectacle: a lizard was chasing an enormous cockroach along one of the beams of the roof. I felt I was on some race track. I began to shout for the lizard. I wanted him to catch up with this horrible insect. He had almost reached it when the stupid cockroach sought shelter under the belly of another animal. It was a huge hairy mygale spider who plunged her teeth in his belly before sucking him like an egg. A few seconds later the empty shell of the cockroach landed on my nose.

It must have been way past midnight when I finally fell asleep. Not for long. Indeed it was still dark when I felt my companion's elbows drumming upon my hips.

"Dominique, let's get up!" he said. "We must run to the latrines now, otherwise we'll have to queue for hours." I looked at my watch, it was only 4:00 A.M.! I'll never forget this early trip to the latrines of the City of Joy. Access was already obstructed by a line of several dozen people. The arrival of a sahib in jeans and basketball shoes provoked a lively upsurge of curiosity and amusement, and all the more so because, in my ignorance of the customs of the country, I had committed an unforgivable blunder: I had brought with me a few sheets of toilet paper. Was it conceivable that anyone should want to preserve in paper a defilement expelled from the body? A young boy came up to me with a tin full of water.

"Take this water, big brother, and wash your bottom with it," he urged me gently.

It was bright daylight when I was back in Kovalski's hovel. The priest had just returned from the fountain with a bucket of water.

"Sorry," he said, "that's all I've got to offer for a shower!" I took the bucket and squatted in the alleyway outside the hovel. I was in the process of vigorously scrubbing my toes with the local soap, a mixture of ashes and mud, when the elderly Hindu from the teashop opposite called out to me in horror.

"Sahib, that's not how you're supposed to wash yourself. It's your head you should wash first, and your feet last, after you have cleaned everything else." I was about to stammer some excuse for committing this new sacrilege when a beautiful little girl with a yellow flower in her hair appeared in front of me. The vision of a half-naked sahib sprinkling himself with water amused her so much that she burst out laughing.

"Why are you washing yourself anyway?" she asked. "Your skin is already so white!"

And so ended with this unforgettable burst of humor what I like to remember as "my worst but also most rewarding travel experience."

Thousand and Two Nights

by Pico Iyer

"I CAN'T SLEEP with a mouse."

"Why not? You've slept with worse. Including me."

"I can't. I wouldn't get a wink of sleep."

"Then you won't be sleeping with a mouse," I said with infantile logic.

Kristin was on her first budget-trip ever, and suffering the consequences of a Stockholm background and a job organizing tours in five-star hotels. I was a teenager at Oxford writing a thesis on lewdness in the plays of John Webster. We were in a $3-a-night room in the middle of Cairo, equipped with walk-up elevators, curdled goats' milk, and a team of men more than ready to follow up on the leers and propositions that had greeted us at the airport. The mouse, we gathered, was the closest we'd get to a mini-bar.

Glad to put some distance between us and the small gray corpse (who also filled in for the carpet, the TV, and the telephone), we hurried out into the spicy dark, fragrant evening with the strange enchantments of a *Thousand and One Nights* (a translated copy of which I had in my hand). We entered a restaurant nearby, eulogized by guidebooks, and found it to be manned, so to speak, almost entirely by cats. Service was slow, and standards were uncertain. We wondered whether the cats might pay $3 for a night in a mouse-filled room, and let us sleep on the restaurant floor.

We sauntered back toward our hotel. A man came up to us with a smile.

"Would you like hashish?" he asked me. "Would you like to ride camels tonight, while the moon is full?" I said nothing. "Would you like girls?" he went on, as if Kristin weren't there. "Let me take you to my tent in the desert."

"Okay," I said, in the infinite wisdom of my nineteen years.

"And in return you can give me your woman?"

An even worse deal than a room with mouse included. If this was the Arabian nights, I wished that Scheherezade would stop talking.

The next day, we went to the Pyramids.

"Come," said a tiny wizened fellow in a dirty gallabea. "I will show you the mysteries of our ancient civilization."

He led us into a dark and empty room, and eagerly motioned for me to clamber down a ladder into an even darker and emptier room. When I emerged, it was to find him pinning Kristin to the wall, his eyes set on the mysteries of modern civilization. "You enjoyed the room?" he asked me without shame. "We have many other rooms like that."

We quit the monuments of history and went into a gallabea shop. "Come, let me show you my most special treasures," said the proprietor, leading Kristin away while his brother plied me with mint tea. Five minutes later, Kristin emerged from the changing room, changed indeed, with a tousled gallabea-man behind her.

The next day, we hired a car to take us to Memphis. Hurtling at impossible speeds through tiny villages crammed with animals and children, the driver sent a little boy flying through the air. He bundled the little boy into the back seat, dropped us off at a hospital, and reappeared an hour or so later, with blood all over the floor, anxious to resume the tour. Luckily, we only learned later (after enjoying tea and consolation at the hands of wonderfully solicitous nurses) that in such situations it is often the custom for all those in the car to be held responsible for the accident, and treated accordingly.

Seeking a refuge from such mysteries, we went to dinner with a long-time English resident whose name had been given to us by a former Ambassador. "He's quite a character," we had been told. He lived up to his billing by lecturing us on the pleasures of local catamites.

And so we left Cairo, and fled for the calm of Upper Egypt. On the train to Luxor, a suave young man approached us—a soldier, a sophisticate, a sympathetic ear as we told him about the unexpected hands-on experiences we'd encountered. How sad, he said, and then asked if we could play backgammon for the hand of poor Kristin.

We spent the night in a hotel across from a ruin near Thebes that had been recommended to us by the ex-Ambassador. It cost $1 a night, and was expensive at the price. "But at school," I said, "we read all about the 'soft beds of the East' that seduced Mark Antony!"

"Maybe," said Kristin, "he was a mouse-lover."

The next morning we went out to explore the Valley of the Kings. "Keep an eye out for the Nubians," the proprietor of the hotel called out as we set off. Luckily, the Nubians were keeping an eye out for us. As soon as we entered, a very large man in a gallabea pointed Kristin to a corner. Inexplicably, there were no lechers or exhibitionists in attendance for her there. While she was peering out into the darkness, however, the man grabbed me by the hand, whisked me down a corridor, and tried to assault me. The only meager consolation for my partner as she went through her daily harassment was that I was getting it too: his-and-hers molestation round the clock.

If I recall all this a little flippantly, it is only because both of us were so innocent then that we were all but impervious to the dangers and horrors around us; so innocent, in fact, that we took this to be the way of the world, into which we were being initiated. We were like Yogi and Boo-Boo in the Marabar Caves. Besides, the worse our suffering, the better the stories we could inflict on our friends back home. The one great glory of traveling is that hardship is always redeemed by commotion recollected in tranquillity.

Much later, and in very different circumstances (traveling with my mother), I would find Egypt an incomparably relaxing and accommodating place: gracious and sharp and civil. But traveling in one's teens, on a shoestring budget, with a blue-eyed Swedish blonde, in an Islamic country where blondes are taken to be advertisements of foreign availability, is like walking topless through Times Square.

As our trip went on, we gradually came to know all the varieties of irreligious experience: the guards who smilingly led us into deserted courtyards in Karnak, and invited us to make whoopee there; the guides who wanted to be taken on guided tours of Western permissiveness; the men who offered us camel rides with the camels doing the riding. As I read to Kristin from Lawrence Durrell's sumptuous descriptions of silken decadence in the Alexandria of Cavafy, she looked increasingly put out.

Finally, we learned how to protect ourselves better. On one of our last nights in the country, we went, for refuge, to the lobby of the Nile Hilton, then the most luxurious hotel in Cairo. As soon as we sat down, a man came over and sat down across from us, fixed his eyes on Kristin and let his hands creep down his body.

"Ah, these Egyptians," said a Jordanian businessman, coming to our rescue. "They don't understand that foreign ways are different. Here, let me take you to the disco." Three hours later, he was trying to get Kristin to do the hootchy-kootchy with him in return for a gallabea.

Finally, we were ready to leave. We went to Cairo International Airport, and proceeded to the departure lounge. At last, the world we knew: English families returning from their holidays; international businessmen; a large American buried in a copy of *Time* magazine. We fell into conversation with the American—a teacher from a prep-school in Massachusetts. He told us that he knew the perfect place to stay in Athens: cheap, well-located, seldom full.

We arrived at the Athens airport, and went with him in a taxi to the sleaziest brothel under the Acropolis. Given the absence of dead rodents on the floor, however, we checked in with alacrity. Since it was December 31st, our new friend told us, we should meet at 9:00 P.M., and see in the New Year in style. We met at 9:00, in the joyless bar of some anonymous hotel, and saw in the New Year listening to the teacher's tales of couples he'd spent nights with. His eyes were fixed on me, but he wasn't averse, he implied, to package deals; even honeymoon couples had enjoyed their nights with him.

The next day, feeling less and less like a honeymoon couple, Kristin and I boarded a bus for the three-day trip, through blasted Yugoslavia and snow-drifts in Switzerland, and over a turbulent Channel, back to Oxford. Less than ten days later, just after another international call from the Jordanian businessman (offering two gallabeas now, maybe three), there was a knock at my door. It was the New England teacher, now, by happy chance, employed at a cozy hotel just five miles outside Oxford. He could offer us a great deal on a honeymoon suite, he said: He could help us forget all we'd suffered at the hands of barbarians in the wild and lawless East.

The Dirt on Mudbaths

by Alice Kahn

I AM AN obsessive compulsive traveler. I love travel so much that I spend as much time in anticipation as I do in discovery. For a weekend three hours from my home I will read every book on some overplayed tourist spot like Carmel and come up with an itinerary that is uniquely mine. My husband calls me a Ph.D. in travel.

That's easy for him to say. Although we were both born in Chicago, we've completely opposite travel histories. His: He went everyfuckingplace. Monuments, parks, industrial tours, our nation's capital, on the El Capitan from Chicago to Los Angeles in 1948 where he saw Indians approach the train selling blankets in Albuquerque. Mine: Nothing. Nada. Not one second outside the city until I was fifteen. And I'm talking the real inner city, that challenging pit so culturally exotic to suburban children. As a result, I can recall every detail of the first time I left town, from the bacon at the Illinois Central Station in downtown Chicago to the way the light hit Moore's Mudbath Resort in Waukesha, Wisconsin, as we approached it on foot from the train stop on a summer's day in 1958.

In those days when a sleepover at a friend's was still unusual—who had a spare mattress, a sleeping bag, her own room?—my best friend Penny Kurtz and her mother Tootsie Kurtz invited me to join them for a weekend away. *Away.* On a train! Out of the city, out of the state, to distant, mysterious Wisconsin.

My memory of the "resort" is of a grand, federal-style villa on the order of Marienberg or Montecatini-Terme. Hopefully, the place has been torn down so no one can speak for the veracity of recovered memory. My intellect suspects that the now sophisticated traveler who was that teenage girl was actually looking at some dilapidated relic of the 1920s as filtered through the Great Depression.

At any rate it was surrounded by the kind of green stuff they now call "open space" that I would have assumed was Sherwood Forest at that time. It had something I had only seen in Marx Brothers' comedies called "shuffleboard." It had rooms with beds and little sinks just like in a movie. And it had the "mud room."

There were two rooms actually, a mens and a ladies. Mens and Ladies, Dames and Gents, Buoys and Gulls. In my quite limited world of city parks and restaurants it could only mean one thing.

But, I was to learn, the mud rooms were not bathrooms in the sense I understood the word but actual bath rooms, places where one *bathed*. And not in water but in actual mud. Jeez, I used to do a version of that myself when I was a kid and I usually got in trouble for it. Here, old people paid nurse-like attendants to do what comes naturally to every three-year-old.

There was more to it, Penny and I learned in that long night in the lobby with a pizza-faced, adolescent male desk clerk. Since the average age of the visitors to the resort was about seventy, he was hot stuff. In this world, Tootsie Kurtz was a major babe. The clerk introduced us to the local cuisine, Ritz crackers and cheddar, and he told us the obscene details of the mud ritual.

The reason, he explained, for separate mens and ladies, was that the bather lay nude on a marble slab and—for reasons that perhaps a Russ Meyer or a surviving Mitchell Brother could now explain—the mud was placed over the entire body from the neck down except the genitals and the female breasts.

Unworldly as I was, this negative of the way things should be—genitals covered, everything else exposed—hot-wired my imagination. I spent the night picturing what it must look like, the women with only their breasts and "down there" exposed, the men with only their "things" out.

In the morning Penny and I, bored by now with the octogenarian nature of social life at Moore's Mudbath Resort and desperately missing the acne-enhanced night clerk, launched a plan of action, an idea simple in execution but rich in possibilities.

We switched the mens and ladies signs.

We hid near the entrances as the first elderly gentleman in his robe and slippers, leaning on his hand-carved, wooden cane, went into the mens mud room under the misimpression that he was heading for a roomful of penises resting on mud mounds. We heard the screams, the shrieks, the wild cacophony of immobilized women on marble.

Since then I have taken the mud myself. From Calistoga, California, to the Dead Sea, I have loved the mud. But never will I experience the Felliniesque potential for mud mayhem again.

Borderline Blues (with Herpetile)

by Richard Harris

NOGALES GLARED IN the hot pale sunlight of a late winter afternoon. Two small boys took turns tossing strips of orange peel into the United States. One peeked around the other, as if from behind a stone pillar, at the Mexican border guards in the shack a few meters away, with their pearl-handled .45 pistols. They were absorbed in dividing up a bag of fast food from the Mc-Donald's on the American side and did not notice.

Nogales is a minor port of entry used mostly by fruit and vegetable trucks. Factories on the Mexican side make caskets and colorfully speckle-painted kitchen sinks. The Ferrocarril Pacifico passenger train from Mazatlan and Guadalajara reaches the end of the line within walking distance of the border. There is no bridge to cross, and no river marks the dividing line between the two nations. There are only customs check points on both sides of a chain-link fence.

Backpack slung over one shoulder, I walked past the little mailbox with the sign saying it was the last chance to dispose of any contraband drugs before going through U.S. Customs. I stepped inside.

The customs agent was a gangly man. His wrists shot way out of the gray uniform shirt sleeves. His eyes gleamed with the deep-sunken intensity of a tent revival preacher.

I handed him my passport and showed him what I was bringing back from Mexico. Not much. A Panama hat and a liter of a honey-and-anise liqueur called Xtabentun, which the Mayan people use as an aphrodisiac. These items were tip-offs that I had been to distant regions. In an Arizona voice that sounded somewhat like Roy Rogers facing off with outlaws, he said, "How long did you say you been in Mexico?"

"Nine weeks. Almost ten, since right after Christmas."

"What you been doing down there all this time?"

"Well, I've been traveling around on the trains. I'm writing a book about how to see Mexico by train."

"You say you're a writer? Let's see what you're working on."

"Well, I mean, I haven't written the actual manuscript just yet. I'm only bringing back notes."

"That's fine, son. Let's see them."

"Why do you want to see them? They're just notes."

"Son, there's people that have no visible means of support, and sometimes they claim to be writers when the truth is they're doing—something else. You know what I'm saying? Now, I'm going to ask you once more."

Nodding slowly, I produced from the depths of my pack a leather-bound notebook with divider pockets full of maps, train schedules, business cards, and such. He opened it at random and examined a page, then started flipping through the rest of the notebook. He stopped. The contents of one of the divider pockets wriggled.

A tiny lizard poked its head over the lip of the pocket. The agent laid my notebook on the countertop and bent down to look more closely as the jade-colored reptile the size of a baby's thumb crawled out into the light. Its tail was a snapped-off stump.

Slowly and deliberately, the agent locked his eyes on mine and said, "Now son, I don't know if you're aware of it, but importing a herpetile into the United States without a license is a federal offense punishable by fine and/or imprisonment."

"Herpetile?" I said, "I've never seen that lizard before in my life."

A flicker of amusement twitched the toothpick in the corner of his mouth but did not reach his eyes.

"That's what they all say. Now, what we're going to do is, you're going to remove the contents from your pack one item at a time and place everything on the counter."

"Really. It must have just crawled into my bag. Probably down in Nayarit."

"Son, lay your property out on the counter." He sounded like he meant it. There would be no more nonsense, unless it was official government nonsense.

I started to unload my pack. Squeeze bottles of suntan lotion, shampoo, and insect repellent in a plastic bag. A dog-eared copy of *The People's Guide to Mexico*. Used socks.

"Anyway, it's not my lizard, see, and it's fine with me if you toss it back over the border." And my palm-sized microcassette recorder. As I pulled it out, I pushed the record button. One never knows when a secret tape might come in handy.

"Don't forget them side pockets, either."

A purple pen. Two AA batteries. An empty film canister. A Swiss Army knife.

"How about if I take the lizard back to Mexico? I'll give it to those kids, they can put it on the next train south."

"Can't do that. No, sir. Now we got to get a biologist all the way down here from the university in Tucson to figure out whether this critter is an endangered species or not. Turns out he is, we got to make arrangements with the Mexicans to return him to his place of origin. See what I mean?"

He picked up the miniature cassette recorder. Although it was virtually soundless, he seemed to sense by touch that it was running. His face changed. He looked as if he were about to tell me that I disappointed him, but instead the words that came out were, "Meanwhile, I'd say you've got a problem. I want you to step into that first office down the hall on your right. Leave your property here, we're going to bring in a dog."

"Hey, now wait a minute. I didn't even know that lizard was...."

"You have the right to remain silent. If you waive that right, anything you say can and will...."

My mouth snapped shut. Apparently, surreptitious tapes have a drawback or two.

"That's fine, son," he said. "Now, there's legal requirements that have got to be taken care of. It's going to take a few hours, so you best make yourself comfortable. Your little tape is going to show regulations being followed to the letter. If at my discretion a determination is made that the importation of the herpetile in question was merely incidental to the primary purposes of your trip, well, then you'll be required to sign an affidavit ... uh ...."

My gaze followed his just in time to see the tiny lizard take a flying leap from the counter edge and shoot halfway across the room, where it landed skittering fast on speckled tile floor. Pandemonium followed.

I suddenly became aware that three other agents had gathered to watch the herpetile smuggler get busted. They swung into action like a well-oiled machine. Paper bags appeared. They lunged with the bags at spots where the lizard had been an instant before.

There was shouting back and forth: "I got him!" "No, wait!" "There he goes!" "Watch it, now, watch it!" "Over there!" The lizard dashed behind a file cabinet. Two of the agents moved the cabinet while a third grabbed into space behind it but came up empty.

The corner of my eye caught a flash of green shooting toward the door. The first agent, who had apprehended me, pounced with his brown paper bag—and found himself staring at the knees of a heavy-set Mexican woman with hair the color of steel.

"Ropa," she smiled, holding her meager bundle.

The agent got to his feet and dusted his uniform. The other three stopped what they were doing and watched him. When he had recovered a little dignity, he turned to me.

"Looks like this is your lucky day, son. Pack up your gear, now."

"What about the lizard?"

"Which lizard you talking about? I don't see any lizard. What about that tape?"

I noticed that he still had my passport. He waggled it and gave me a quizzical look.

It seemed like a fair trade to me.

Not in Kansas Anymore

by Joe Gores

BAD TRAVEL EXPERIENCE? Listen, any trip you walk away from in one piece is a winner. Still, I remember one time....

~

"Oh, yes indeed. Very fine. Yes," said the Asian in the little travel agency on Nairobi's Kenyatta Boulevard. He had a pale blue turban and gold teeth. "Everything will be arranged, Very fine first class travel."

It was 1964 and after living three years in Kenya I took first class travel to be an oxymoron on the order of military intelligence. But by steamer down the Nile seemed a wonderfully fitting way to leave the Africa I loved so much.

"You're sure we'll be in Juba before the steamer leaves?"

He was hurt to his very soul.

"But you have my word of honor, oh yes indeed. You shall be arriving in Juba Tuesday night. You shall be sleeping aboard the steamer until it shall be departing Thursday afternoon. What shall be going awry?"

What indeed? Four Europeans (all Americans, but all *wasungu*; white people were "Europeans" in the East Africa of those days), were thrown together for the journey overland from Nairobi through Uganda to the southern Sudan village of Juba. Thence by steamer down (up?) the Nile—it flows north, so directions on it always seem confusing—to Khartoum (famous for Lord Gordon and whirling dervishes and the cavalry charge led by Winnie Churchill), then lazy weeks paddle-wheeling down the Nile to Cairo past the ruins of Egypt's great civilizations. By air to London. As the Brits would say, Bob's your uncle.

But at the Sudanese border we learned that the smoldering civil war between the Moslem Arab northerners and the Christian African southerners had flared into open warfare—something our friendly travel agent had forgotten to tell us about. Like the Mafia, we were assured, the warring factions only killed each other; but still, just to be absolutely safe, road traffic to Juba had to travel in convoys led by military vehicles, with a soldier riding on the roof of each car.

Oh.

Our red, dust-choked, little caravan moved so slowly through the arid acacia thorn scrubland that we arrived after the car ferry across the Nile to Juba was through running for the night. The soldiers made themselves campfires, and broke out the *posho* and *pombe*—white corn mush and beer made out of fermented honey—and as an afterthought posted sentries. We put our sleeping bags out beside the van and went to bed hungry.

No matter. Tomorrow, the Nile steamer. Staterooms. Food.

∾

A rifle shot, screams and shouts brought us upright in the cool pre-dawn air. Then, laughter. I scuttled over to the soldiers' encampment, came back to report: An *ascari* had taken his rifle to bed with him and shot himself in the foot. Hilarious.

Crossing the Nile by the hand-drawn car ferry took the morning, the ferrymen singing scatological songs about their passengers as they hand-over-handed us along the pulley ropes. But we were not rushed; the steamer wouldn't be leaving until tomorrow afternoon.

The van dumped us and our backpacks in the middle of the dusty town square and disappeared. Hungry as we were, we went directly to the ferry office. A beaming African official in wilted khakis and a red fez awaited us.

"The ferry? Ah, assuredly, gentlemens and ladies, it shall arrive Thursday." He pointed at the calendar. "Thursday, a week. Too early in the season sah."

"Thursday a week," I said in an unbelieving voice.

"Or surely the week after, sah."

Something else our friendly travel agent had forgotten to tell us: the Nile steamers weren't running yet. We counted money. Food, a cheap hotel.

No hotel, cheap or expensive, and very little food. Juba was jammed with stranded travelers, the rebels had interdicted the road north. By the next day they had closed the road south. All plane flights out already were over-booked. And hundreds of refugees fleeing from the civil war in the Congo (not quite christened Zaire yet) were arriving everyday.

We broke into an abandoned white hunter's office—nobody came to Sudan to hunt anymore—spread our sleeping bags on the concrete floor, and found we could scrounge a meal a day at the refugee camp set up on the bank of the Nile. In darkness, we fell into exhausted sleep.

The thunder of 3:00 A.M. gunfire woke us.

"Get up!" I yelled. "They're attacking the town!"

Our walls were thick, we were relatively safe. But no bullets seemed to be hitting the windows. We edged cautious eyes up over the sills. All looked peaceful; outside was only moonlight. But the sounds of gunfire continued.

I slipped out for a *recce*, and returned sheep-faced. At the bakery down the street, they shook the huge aluminum sheets on which they baked bread for the refugee camp to clean off the flour; it sounded just like gunfire.

Two days later, we learned the steamer would not be coming at all; and the refugees from the Congo had begun fleeing back *into* the Congo, a sure indication that bad times were abrewing.

After ten days, with the last of our money we managed to bribe the pilot of an old C-47 Dakota flying in supplies to take us back with him to Nairobi— whence we had started. I chased our friendly travel agent around his desk for a refund. We never got it, but did finally get airplane tickets for the four of us to London. We had our own air tickets from there.

~

I arrived in New York with eight dollars in my pocket. Since I was owed $250 by *Manhunt* Magazine for a story of mine they had published months before, I went up to their Fifth Avenue office and chased their editor around his desk.

But that's another story entirely, isn't it?

I Think Our Driver Is Stoned: The Slow Road from Istanbul to Herat

by Rick Steves

It was 1978, a year before the rise of Khomenei, the war in Afghanistan, and the publication of the first edition of *Europe Through the Back Door.* Walking past Istanbul's legendary Pudding Shop, the traditional hippie springboard for overland treks to Kathmandu, Gene and I were heading for a Turkish bath.

Leaving my money belt and all first world advantages in my cubicle, holding a tattered wrap around my waist and walking gingerly across slippery marble into the steamy netherlands of Turks under Byzantine domes, I felt a little nervous. After an awkward sit in the sauna, my Turk, who doled out massages like a cannery worker gutting salmon, put me onto the round marble slab and I looked up at sunrays piercing the domed roof.

With a loud slap on my chest he landed on me, like hands kneading dough in a prison bakery. He smashed and stretched my tight muscles. He rolled me belly down for the joint stretching. Bouncing my feet to my back, walking on me, cracking my neck with enough power to break it, he was a credit to his trade. Gene and I, laying naked on our bellies, ears pressed to the marble, grimaced and groaned in each other's face, reassuring each other that our masseur must know the breaking point. Then, like gumbies with lobotomies, we were led to marble thrones to be doused in hot water and scrubbed with brillo-pad mittens.

Clean and optimistic, we were on our way to Herat, a town in Afghanistan. Smug as two worldly twenty-four-year-olds could be, with seat reservations sixteen and seventeen in hand, we marveled at the uncivilized riot for bus seats. Tossing our rucksacks to the man on the bus rooftop, we boarded. Last on, it became clear—to our horror—that seat reservations had no meaning. Two seats remained: after-thought seats hanging over the rear stairwell, the only ones on the bus that didn't recline, and the only pair that moved forward at each bus stop.

Bouncing bolt upright out of Istanbul, we took stock of our situation. Our commander in chief looked like a Barbary pirate, complete with exposed hairy chest, bandanna, and a huge scar between his handlebar mustache and ear. Sitting atop a rear wheel, we had maximum noise and bounce with minimum leg room. The smelly engine behind us rumbled and functioned as a heater stuck on high. Our reading lights didn't work, and my seat came complete with a sharp point and nasty screw. We were surrounded by smokers, the window didn't open, and cigarette ash blew in my face. Getting up to stretch my legs, the pirate eyeballed me in his mirror and shouted, "Mister, sit down."

Only sixty-two more hours.

Well into the night, Gene and I decided to crack open the bon voyage bottle of Bulgarian cognac our friends in Sofia had given us a few days earlier. Made bolder by several big glasses of scotch served by the Iranians across the aisle, we eventually finished the cognac and fell asleep.

Ripped out of a deep sleep by the pirate's hysterical screams, I snapped awake just as the back-up driver was grinding over the curb and crashing to a noisy stop. Smoke billowed, belongings flew everywhere. I thought we were on fire and my still woozy head played out a worst case scenario.

We all filed out to inspect the damage as the cold night wind blew fiercely. The pirate was screaming at his back-up man. Turkish grease monkeys climbed under the rear end, small boys appeared out of nowhere with tea and bread rings, and I found a chunk of ground clean enough to continue my night's sleep.

Most of the next day was spent drinking tea, snoozing, washing under a hose, and getting to know the rest of the people on the bus. Only one member of our four-man Iranian crew could drive a bus. The pirate would pilot the rest of the trip solo and we'd have no more overnight rides. Gene and I, the only Americans on board, seemed pretty green compared to our well-traveled bus mates. Brits, French, Belgians, a Russian, an Iranian student, Muslim women and children rounded out the gang.

A day later the bus was repaired and we continued our eastbound journey. Checking our progress on the Turkey to India overland map draped over our two seats, we were disheartened. At midnight the driver stopped and found us hotels. We shared a room with a Belgian couple. My sheet was littered with the hairs and scent of the previous occupant. When I complained about my dirty linen to the hotel man he immediately rushed up, apologized, and turned it over.

The following morning our driver roused us out of bed at 5:00 A.M. (we thought departure time was at 7:00 A.M.) and dragged me, by my hair, onto the bus. By mid-afternoon we stopped by a riverside. The pirate stripped to his underpants and with soap in hand, went for a bath and a swim. Like a wild kid he rolled in the sand and splashed back into the river. Then our driver urged everyone by insisting, "No bath, no Tehran." We were slow to catch on but eventually all the men were floating down the refreshing river in their underwear.

As we piled back on the bus I scored a point with the driver by offering a piece of honeydew melon and he responded by putting the pedal to the metal. Our border crossing into Iran was uneventful and by 10:00 P.M. we barreled into Tabriz just in time to witness the armored riot squads readying themselves for another bout of student trouble. The Shah was about to fall.

Nobody wanted to sleep in Tabriz, and a cheer rose as we picked up a second driver who took us through the night to Tehran. Our visit coincided with a major Muslim holiday and all transportation to the holy town of Meshad was booked for several days. We bivouacked in Amir Kabir, the vagabond hotel district, where everyone heading down the freak road to India killed time. Hidden behind piles of tires and greasy auto parts were countless budget hotels decorated with smashed bugs, broken windows, cigarette butts stuck in sooty holes in the walls, and bare, dangling, twenty-watt light bulbs. There we sat, exhausted, methodically pinching bugs on our legs.

When we finally arrived in Meshad, we boarded another eastbound bus. At the Iran-Afghanistan border the government welcomed everyone to an interesting museum featuring the prison careers of drug smugglers. There was no admission charge.

After zipping through customs, we walked across a windy desert to no man's land. In the shade of a wrecked and rusted VW, we peeled an apple and waited for the bank and the doctor's office to open. Gene was missing a shot. No problem, they were delighted to inject him on the spot. I'll always remember the needle bending as a nurse tried to force its blunt tip into Gene's flesh.

With customs formalities completed, we flew off down the good road to Herat. Suddenly a commotion broke out in the front of the bus. The Afghanis decided to double the price of the ride. We principled road-to-India travelers refused. When a leathery Afghan pulled out a knife that could fillet a goat, panic broke out. A Pakistani urged us to pay the bribe but we worried that would merely lead to further extortion. Compromising, we agreed to pay a fifty percent arrival bonus in Herat.

Later that day our bus stopped at a desolate tea shop with a well and a bunch of locals skinning a still warm goat. The tea house was classic Afghanistan with old, traditionally wrapped men, who looked like hard workers but never seem to do anything but sit around on rugs drinking tea and smoking hashish. The room filled with smoke and their glassy dark eyes smiled. I joined them along with several other passengers. The word spread—our driver and his crew were stoned.

Back on the hot bus we finally made it to Herat. We checked into the best hotel in town—where locals celebrate their weddings. The menu featured marked down prices and an explanatory note: "Since the People's Revolution, all prices are lowered by ten afs."

Standing on our balcony, we surveyed our fascinating destination. It was one of those small epiphanies that makes every traveler proud. Flower-bedecked, torch-lit, horse-drawn chariots charged through the streets past soldiers and police guarding the recent revolution. An elderly cleaning man stood on the next balcony admiring the sunset. I told him we needed some toilet paper. Watching the sun melt behind the purple mountains he turned to us and said, "Yes, it is very beautiful."

Maddening Madagascar

by Lisa Alpine

THE PROSTITUTES THOUGHT our son was a real gentleman. In fact, maybe the only gentleman (besides his father), in the crowd, dining al fresco in front of the Hotel du France in Antananarivo.

This was our first night in the capital of Madagascar after a flight from Nairobi. At the suggestion of a fellow world traveler, we added this obscure stop onto a safari trip in Kenya.

It took awhile for us to realize that these well-heeled, Levi-clad, young girls milling around us in the restaurant were plying their trade. Packs of hungry-eyed children clustered beyond the iron fence separating us from the sidewalk. The girls would pass food and money to the youngsters—family members waiting to be fed.

While the girls waited for men to consign their services, they bounced our blue-eyed, blond-haired, three-year-old on their knees. Cutest Westerner they'd ever seen!

When we bedded down in our room, haunting sounds of creaking springs and frequent groans seeped through the walls accenting the muggy night. Sleep eluded us as deep male grunts kept us awake and confirmed our suspicions that this hotel was not on the Relais et Chateaux route.

At 6:00 A.M., the following morning, we were shuffled to the train station and sent out to explore the mysteries of Madagascar in a nineteenth-century iron horse. Late in the day we disembarked at Perinet, on the edge of a lemur preserve, and checked into a dilapidated hotel next to the train station.

One of the wonders that lured us here was the prolific flora and fauna unique to Madagascar. This bright red earth island 250 miles off the coast of East Africa is the place to find grotesquely shaped Baobab trees swollen like elephant's legs, mysterious underwater coelacanths and the mouse lemur, the smallest primate in the world.

It's not easy to see these uncommon, wild creatures, and exotic growths—they aren't just hanging out at the side of the road waiting to sign autographs. We worked to see nature's wonders!

A guide led us into the rain forest looking for indri-indri, one of thirty-three lemur species found only in Madagascar. Treading for miles beneath the dense canopy we craned our necks looking for this endangered, elusive (it sleeps eighteen hours a day) lemur. Finally, several indri-indri stirred the leafy roof a hundred feet above us for a brief glimpse of furry behinds.

The next morning my husband felt the lure of the lemur and took off again with the guide into the yawning green. My son and I chose to explore a local village. We found a town near the train tracks and were soon surrounded by a swarm of children—jaundiced, with bloated stomachs and brittle hair. Sewage trickled down the gullies beside the dirt track that wound through town. I held onto my son, who wanted to pass out candy. How do you pass out twenty-five pieces of candy to hundreds of children?

My husband found me crying at the hotel. It broke my heart to see children in such a hopeless situation while my robust son, wrapped protectively in my arms, reached out to them, wanting to share his candy stash.

That night we boarded a train for the ten hour ride to Tamatave, a town under martial law. Rumors spread through the train that just the day before Malagasy had rioted against Hindu residents, killing many, and exiling three hundred. To add to our discomfort, torrential sheets of rain pounded on the steamy windows. There was no food, water, electricity, or ventilation. The windows were rusted shut. Only the lightning bolts illuminated the train interior at night.

Desperate for a breath of fresh air, I disembarked at one stop and stood in the pouring rain refusing to get back on. My husband grabbed my arm and yanked me onto the train as it began to move away from the platform. Finally the train came to the end of the line.

We stayed in another whorehouse. It seemed all the "decent" hotels were bordellos. We were beginning to wonder where the other tourists were. Hadn't met one yet. By the end of the three week trip we had encountered a handful: two French expats from the nearby island of Reunion and three Russian scientists on leave from their expedition boat. After the French colonists left Madagascar in 1960, the country went Marxist, and closed its doors to Westerners. The doors were beginning to creak open again, and it seems we were some of the first tourists allowed in.

It was hard to ignore all the broken shop windows downtown from the rioting of the day before as we drove through Tamatave. We were flying to Isle Saint Marie, a coconut strewn haven away from civilized madness! An island cloaked in romantic history, the retirement spot for legendary pirates.

We boarded the small plane thinking it was our escape toward a real vacation. We headed into a tormented, bruised, blue sky. The wind god played ping-pong with our aircraft. I crossed myself, I'm not Catholic, but it beat biting off my nails. Touch down we did though, right before I threw up. Nobody got off the plane but us, yet people were milling to get on. We quickly learned a cyclone was coming, adding another lesson to our education of firsts. Cyclones are very noisy, like a lion roaring in your ear nonstop. And wet. And they last several days. We were stuck staring at the downpour with our ears plugged for four days. Not a shred of blue sky. At night we slept under the bed on the concrete floor just in case the roof blew off and lifted our son off like in *The Wizard of Oz*. On a positive note, an unlimited amount of lobster was served for lunch and dinner.

We finally got off Isle Sainte Marie, but things did not improve as we continued on our journey. One of our worst days involved a twelve-hour ride over a lavishly pot-holed dirt road, in 100-degree heat sitting on leaky gasoline cans. My husband suffered the most as his skin was carpeted with a red rash from eating too much lobster. The driver dropped us off in Ambanja, a town with no motorized vehicles in sight. The streets were a swirl of livestock animals, saronged women, men with wary eyes, and throngs of children. It was too hot to be inside at night. Charcoal braziers smoked in front of huts. Our lodging was a dive, but they had beer! Beer was our savior, or should I compare it to an anesthetic, or sanity buffer? We sat on rickety chairs in the middle of the road swigging Three Horses beer and watching our son cavort with a baby goat. I felt happy, ecstatic even (maybe the gasoline fumes that enveloped us in the car affected me). It was worth the horrendous ride to this remote pageant of humanity milling before us swathed in bright colors, dark skin glowing from the fire light. The beer not only went to my head, it went to my bladder. I giddily walked to the outhouse and entered in pitch dark. I heard a scurrying noise, and clumsily turned on my flashlight. Two fat rats with glowering eyes brazenly eyed my bare descending bottom. I felt too sick to even scream.

The mosquitoes in this region of Madagascar are chloro-quine resistant and we couldn't give our son the other anti-malarial drug, Fansidar, because it is too strong for children (and probably adults). If one of the several hundred constantly hovering bugs bit our son, he had a high probability of get-ting malaria. We were on mosquito (and rat) alert all night. Bzzzzz, swat. Bzzzzz, swat. Bzzzz, swat.

The next morning we waited with others at an inlet for a boat to Hell-Ville on the island of Nosy Be, Madagascar's only touted tourist beach resort. The town's name made me queasy. Why was it named after the Devil's abode? This was the only English town name we had encountered. I wondered what the Malagasy names stood for ... Tamatave: *town of broken glass* maybe, or Ambanja: *land of ass-biting rats?* A white-washed steamer pulled up after the prerequisite half-day tardiness. The ocean was smooth as glass ("calm before a storm?" I mulled). Dolphins broke the placid emerald surface. An immi-grant Chinese family offered us sticky buns and tea.

In Chinese-accented French, they told me how the sister boat of the one we were on had sunk a month before "right over there." They all turned and pointed. There she was stick-ing her nose up out of the water! "Everybody died. Too many passengers for old boat. Like today ... too many." They seemed calm. Why should I worry? They're not. I started counting heads and clenched my jaw with every tilt of the boat.

Finally Nosy Be appeared on the horizon and we hadn't sunk yet. We docked in Hell-Ville. We checked into a Holiday Inn no less! Clean towels, French cuisine, movies at night. Ironically, the place with the most foreboding name turned out to be normal. I was bored. Sitting on the beach with no major catastrophe to wrinkle my brow seemed so dull.

By the way, I made none of this up and left out half. My memory could not spit out every traumatic detail. Some days in Madagascar I was on cruise control just so I wouldn't go out of my mind. Those days I'd write murder mysteries in my head, pray for a cold beer, and clean my finger nails. It's the simple pleasures that started to sink in after we'd had our conceptions of vacation pounded out of us. A scraggly crew of Chinese acrobats were in town our last night and for thirty cents we watched them in the front row balancing on top of twenty chairs and doing pretzel-shaped contortions.

Would I go back? *Yes,* but I'd leave my son at home and expect the unexpected. Now that Madagascar has opened up to Westerners maybe it has lost its rough and tumble edge.

My kid, if he could remember, would probably tell you a whole different story. One filled with odd wonders: bug wings the size of his hand, kid goats frolicking with him on the street, and plane rides reminiscent of Mr. Toad's Wild Ride at Disneyland. I'd have a hard time keeping him from coming along.

Tail End

by Suzanne Lipsett

1968. FOR ME, it was the year of living surreally—chaotically—
along the hippie trail. I was twenty-five and, as I see now from
the pinnacle of fifty, stupid as a calf. Who but a calf would set
off happily and hopefully to travel the world with a boy perpetually puzzled by the look in her eyes?

Between Mogadiscio and East Africa, the tension built, and
in Israel, during one of the rainiest winters since the biblical
flood, it grew claws. In Istanbul we began to snap at each
other. We crossed Turkey in furious irritability. And in Teheran
I threw an extended fit; his strategy of choice was dreadful
silence. By India, on the top shelf of a three-tiered sleeping car
on a third-class train, with my head bouncing on a soft corner of my hated, book-stuffed backpack, I pretended to be
traveling alone. And by Nepal, with a lifeless snap, the last of
the love finally came apart like an old, overpulled rubber band.

The next morning I washed my long hair under a pump
in the tiny cobblestone courtyard of a cardboard hippie hotel.
In my bag I had a plane ticket to Calcutta and then on to Bangkok; the ultimate destination was San Francisco. After breakfast in a restaurant world-famed for its hashish brownies, I
took a minivan to the strange little Quonset-hut airport, and
boarded a sixteen-seat plane.

You're not inclined to stand up on a plane like that, for fear
of putting your foot through the floor. I white-knuckled that
flight, but the connecting one to Bangkok took three years off
my life. As the beautiful stewardesses in their whispering silken

saris demonstrated the seatbelt buckle and pointed to the exits, the rolling plane gradually filled with smoke.

"Condensation," whispered my seatmate finally in response to my bulging eyes. "It has something to do with the heat and humidity of Calcutta." By the time the wing dipped over the city and we had begun to climb, you could hardly see the people across the aisle.

The hotel in Bangkok was a huge, ramshackle affair above a ground-floor restaurant that served omelets the size of a sailor's forearm. I checked in on the second floor and made my way up two flights around little groups of people on the stairs. In every corner small children with the heart-melting faces of Asian angels looked after bare-bottomed infants.

In my room, after sleeping the sleep of the dead, I did what any self-respecting grass widow anywhere does to celebrate the end of a dead-end love affair. I stood at the streaky mirror over the streaky sink, and with a single-edged razor blade I had bought at the airport for the purpose, I cut off my long, thick hair. I went from a shoulder-length, sun-bleached mane to a boy cut shaped close around the ears with long bangs and feathery sideburns. After half an hour, I looked back to survey the damage, and I'm sure I smiled at myself in the mirror with a dawning sense of freedom.

Wow. I loved it.

"God, your hair looks terrific. I *adore* the cut."

I was tackling one of the massive omelets downstairs, unconcerned by the distinctive flavor of soapsuds. Mouth full, I looked up at the speaker in surprise.

"We saw you come in last night. You looked exhausted." She was a young, beautiful American woman dressed in a white Indian tunic and pants. A shiny dark plait of hair, loosely braided, hung down her back. Behind her stood a young, beautiful American man, perhaps twenty-five, with one arm wrapped around her shoulders and chest and the other hand holding her arm. "But with that haircut, you're a completely different person."

"Fourteen hours of sleep didn't hurt," I answered.

"Sleep?" cried the young man in a friendly way. "How can you sleep in this place?"

I gestured to them to sit down and with a familiar air they called their order to the cook.

"Listen, I don't even remember lying down. I didn't hear a thing."

"You will, you will," the guy said, laughing. "It's like trying to catch some sleep in one of those porno movie houses—"

"She doesn't know," the woman said to him.

"Know what?" I asked.

"That this place is one huge all-day, all-night whorehouse. They rent the rooms by the half hour."

"Look through the cracks in your wall sometime," said the woman.

"Not that you can help it. The place is just so makeshift—it's not so much cracks as stripes." This amused them both greatly, and their laugh was a dazzling display of American orthodontic success. "Jamie and Shayna," said the man, giving a wave down the table with his free hand and squeezing Shayna's arm with the other. "From Eugene." These kids not only looked like twins, they were apparently joined at the hip.

That night Shayna and Jamie came to my room and pointed out the quarter-inch cracks between the dark green wallboards. Actually, I didn't even have to put my eye to the crack to confirm what they told me: The breathy rumble of a man's voice and the light, fast, piercing interplay of Thai in two—or could it have been three?—women's voices formed a vivid soundtrack. We barely had to look in the direction of the wall to see the scene clearly—lights blazing, clothes flung off, drinks and food abounding. Standing in my room looking and not looking, then running into the hall and down the stairs in hysterics, bound the three of us into one of those instant traveler's friendships.

The next morning, horribly early, Shayna tapped at my door.

"Suzanne." I sat up in bed, not sure whether I'd dreamed or heard my name.

Inside, she crawled next to me and sat with her back against the wall as if she were at a sweet sixteen slumber party. Trusting and open as a child—she was twenty, but seemed much younger—she reached over and stroked my cropped hair.

"I just love it," she told me again.

With a shake of her head she whipped the long plait from her back over her shoulder. Holding it with one hand, she stroked it with the other. "I just love it," she repeated. "Listen, Sue. I need you to do this for me," Shayna said.

"Do what?"

She looked at me hard, clearly assessing my character.

"Listen. Would you promise? Would you not talk to Jamie until later?"

"What are you—?"

"No, really. I just want to ask you this one thing, but I need you to do it now, before you see him. Okay? Would you do this for me?"

"Uh, wait a minute—" What were these two sweet-faced strangers up to, anyway?

"No, listen, it's not anything illegal or anything like that." She sat stroking her plait. Finally she visibly decided to plunge in. "It's just . . . I want you to cut my hair."

I'd cut lots of hair, not just my own.

"Oh, sure. No problem."

She looked like I'd just agreed to take out a contract on her mother.

"But you won't tell Jamie? I mean, I'll pay you and everything—"

"You'll pay me to cut your hair? What am I, a sadist? When do you want to do it?"

She sat silently for a long time, with the heavy braid of hair in her motionless hands. She stared into the middle distance, and it was clear there was a struggle going on. Finally, she whispered, "Right now. Let's do it now."

She sat on the rickety chair in the middle of the room as if she were reaching for a concealed weapon, and brought out a pair of blunt scissors from the pocket of her tunic. With a single sawing cut, I took off the shiny black braid, and it fell heavily to the floor. Then, using a single-edged blade, I razored the rest up close to her head. When I was through she got up and peered into the streaked bureau mirror.

"Shorter," she whispered, and sat down again.

We did it three times. After the second time, I began to get nervous.

"Are you sure you want to do this?" I asked.

"No," she said bluntly.

"Oh, *great*—"

"No, go on. I mean, I'm sure."

So I went over it again, reassuring myself that after all it would grow, and left nothing but a flat dark shiny mat coating the well-shaped head.

"It looks really great," I breathed, relieved. It did. The androgyny of the cut blended with the fresh young-girl beauty to add a touch of mystery.

"Yeah," she said in a tone I couldn't interpret and let herself out of my room.

I had a date with a friend of a friend whom I'd tracked down in the city, and at dusk made my way across Bangkok to a café bar where Jamie and Shayna and I had agreed the night before to meet for dinner. Groups of American servicemen on leave hollered at each other above the sounds of the Rolling Stones and a watery light show played over dancers in various degrees of intoxication. If most of the men were American military men, virtually all of the women were beautiful Thai girls. Though they wore superhigh spiked heels, they all seemed the size of American grade school children, and by contrast the men appeared to be gargantuan.

Across the dance floor I saw Jamie and Shayna at a table, but it was hard for me to tell which was which. Both wore white shirts, and both had their dark cropped heads bent over tall beers.

"Hey," I said as I joined them. Shayna nodded and attempted to smile. Jamie didn't look up.

"So what's up?" I asked them, over brightly.

Wearily, Jamie lifted his head and looked my way. For a moment he didn't speak. Finally he said something I couldn't hear.

Judging from the tragic look on his beautiful face—the crease between the eyes, the drawn-down, black brows over Pacific blue—I didn't want to know, but I asked him to repeat himself anyway.

Above the roar of the music, he shouted, "I said, you ruined her."

Shayna looked away.

"I ruined her?" I repeated dumbly.

"Yes, bitch. You made her into nothing."

Shayna, her face still averted from me, covered her eyes with her hand. I remembered the embrace that had caged her in his arms from behind the first time I met them. If earlier in the day she had resolved to stake a claim to her body by doing what she would with her own hair, by now the resolve had wilted under the onslaught of Jamie's rage. Our on-the-road friendship had burned brightly for a moment, illuminating my prospects for a companionable few days, but it was over now.

"Uh—"

"Look at her. She looks ... she looks"—a note of sheer misery crept into his angry voice. "She looks like a guy."

"Hey, wait a minute, Jamie—" I began, recalling my caution and Shayna's exhortations to cut more.

"Just go away," Jamie snapped over his beer. "Haven't you done enough?"

"Listen—"

He looked up squarely into my face, and I noticed that for the first time since I had seen them together he was making no physical contact with Shayna. In fact, his two hands were side by side on the table, and he appeared to be about to push himself up to stand and confront me more assertively.

"You know, she asked me—"

"Get the hell out of here. I don't want you here," shouted Jamie. I saw that it was useless to argue.

I crossed back over the dance floor. And suddenly, midway, I was engulfed by the beautiful prostitutes. Their perfume pressed in on me, their black eyes pierced me, and—I felt it for some seconds before I actually understood it—their sharp, talon nails scratched at my skin. Blindly, I had ventured into their territory, and I guess they saw me—tall, female, blondish—as encroaching on their trade. The beat of the music covered any words they might have spoken, but suddenly one girl leaned close. "Um-eeri-kan beetch," she hissed distinctly in my ear. I cut her a glance and saw her glaring at me from another planet. She whipped her hand up close to my eyes and opened and closed the red nails of thumb and fingers in a tiny pantomimed threat.

It was the end: the end of my ingenuous attempts to understand the world from a constantly moving vantage point, the end of my resources, and the end of the line. I fell asleep that night to the sounds of an energetic three- or foursome crossing the language barrier and in the morning dug my return ticket to San Francisco out of an inside pocket of my pack. The time would come once or twice when I'd lay a razor blade to my own hair again, but as for setting foot into the minefield between lovers where who knew what lay just below the surface, I was out of the beauty business for good.

Seeking the Mother of Immortal Bliss:
The Temple at Vallickavu

by Naomi Mann

*Dear Mom, my plans have changed. I'll be staying in India
... in a place called Vallickavu....*

VALLICKAVU? I COULD not find Vallickavu on any map. A mere
speck on the Malabar Coast, this tiny fishing village lies hidden deep in the state of Kerala, near the south, westernmost
tip of the Indian subcontinent. Yet to a growing number of
select visitors, Vallickavu is recognized as the headquarters of
the guru Mata Amritanandamayi, the Mother of Immortal
Bliss—a must-see for a new generation of meditation junkies
and religious thrill-seekers, a five-star destination for rever-
ent pilgrims in search of the India beyond Delhi and Agra,
beyond Varanasi and Srinigar, beyond the grasp of the senses.

*I haven't pierced my nose or shaved my head.... Still I am
happier—more at peace—than ever before. To live like a
nun appeals to me very much: simply, with my focus on
spiritual rather than material or worldly or scholarly things.*

Neither adventure nor seeker myself, I went to Vallickavu
to see my daughter. A Jewish mother, secular and agnostic,
until this moment I had never contemplated the quest for
God-consciousness or communion with a Divine Mother of
Bliss. Mobilized by Jessica's first letter from Kerala, armed with
literature on cult awareness and mind control, I was embarked
on a different pursuit, an urgent, even desperate mission of

rescue. At the very least, I needed to see for myself the marvelous teacher, and the magic that held my child spellbound within her enchanted circle.

Amma, Ammachi—or simply Mother, as she is known to her followers, was born there forty years ago as Sudhamani, the daughter of poor fishermen. Reputed from birth to possess prodigious spiritual powers, in her early teens she experienced a blissful epiphany and was hailed as a *sat guru,* a realized master, an object of devotion and worship by the local people.

> *To have a daughter studying in India is one thing—but living in an ashram?! It's every Jewish mother's worst nightmare—right? Yet it's what I wish to do with all my heart....*

As the fame of the girl-saint spread, devotees gathered around her in the Hindu fashion—some for the miracles and the healing, others for the teaching. Most came simply to be touched and embraced by the guru in her unorthodox, uniquely intimate *darshans,* or public audiences. Ammachi licked the wounds of lepers, conjured visions, sprinkled rose petals on barren couples, and blessed the newborns nine months later. Assuming the *bhavana,* the mood and form of Kali or Devi, she sang and danced as if possessed by the goddess. She hugged everyone. She was a sensation.

> *I need a sponsor to renew my visa.... It will not be a university or a school, but the ashram. It's a mission plus an orphanage plus a school ... like a yeshiva combined with a kibbutz?*

Then, in the early '80s, Amma was discovered by Westerners. Drawn by rumors of an Enlightened Being, some came to stargaze, others stayed to adore—and to advise and build. Today, the one-time village prodigy leads a worldwide religious movement with ashrams, schools, worship centers, hospices, and orphanages in sixteen Indian towns and cities, Australia, Japan, Europe, and the United States.

But the heart of Amma's domain remains in Vallickavu, just beyond the clustered fishermen's houses, in a serenely chaotic assemblage of buildings thrown up topsy-turvy under the tall palms on this remote backwater of the Arabian Sea.

To reach Ammachi's ashram, I flew from San Francisco to Taiwan to Bangkok to Delhi to Bombay to Trivandrum, where Jessica and I embraced at last with cautious joy. Exhausted, I asked no questions and formed no image of what might lie ahead as our taxi careened and honked through two hours of steamy heat until it lurched to a stop where both the road and Vallickavu proper ended abruptly at the water's edge.

> I'll write you some other time about tropical Kerala, where coconuts and bananas grow everywhere, and what it's like to wear a five-meter long sari. . . .

I arrived in the twilight of a sultry January night, my first sight, the looming shadows of the huge Chinese fishing nets, crouched eerily over the channel like giant insects. A boat, a sort of shabby gondola crammed with silent, staring passengers, glided slowly towards us, pooled by a boatman who scrutinized us with insolent intimacy.

Jessica tossed our bags into the rank puddles on the floor of the boat, climbed over the side, and reached up to help me in. It took only moments to cross to the opposite shore, to Amma's world, where we clambered out, waded through the lukewarm water to a sandy bank, and started down a narrow path overhung by banana trees. We shared the way with a score of Indian men and women hurrying in the same direction, but I could see no sign of habitation. All was quiet except for

the flap of their sandaled footsteps, and a throbbing or hum-
ming vibration I thought must be the sea.

After about a quarter of a mile, the path turned, and opened
abruptly into a large clearing. Encircling the low buildings that
formed this courtyard were torches, their pungent smoke min-
gling in the semi-darkness with the cloying scent of incense.
What I had earlier understood as the distant crashing of surf,
I could now identify as an immediate and enveloping sound:
the pounding of drums and the rhythmic chanting of many,
many voices. Dozens of silhouetted figures strolled or darted
around us, their white robes glowing in the torch light, a ghostly
embellishment of the other-worldly scene.

> *School holds no interest now. Nor does random travel or a
> career, or so many of the things one might expect to con-
> cern someone like me....*

But most astounding, most exotic, most indescribably
rising before me was the colossal mass of the temple itself,
perhaps a hundred feet high and at least eighty feet wide, an
exuberant hulk dwarfing the simple outbuildings scattered
around it like so many toy houses. Even in the near darkness
I could see that the temple was alive with color, a bright and
zany hodgepodge of blues, yellows, pinks, reds, and greens
splashed from the palette of an intoxicated child. A frieze of
fancifully carved figures—saints and deities I could not name—
girdled the midsection, while others lolled and frolicked on
ledges, or peered down randomly from the extravagant con-
fection.

With my sweaty hand firmly in her grasp, Jessica pulled
me across the courtyard and up a broad flight of stairs to a
spacious landing, a sort of temple ante-room, past groups of
sari and dhoti-clad figures lounging in the murky light, past

hundreds and hundreds of thonged rubber sandals, scattered evidence of the faithful already at worship. We pressed on to a monumental staircase and climbed to a wide balcony where I found myself looking down into an immense hall, 200 feet long and perhaps seventy-five feet wide, dimly lit by flickering electric chandeliers hung from the ceiling soaring six stories above us.

> *My goal is not to escape or run away from anything. Nor is it some flaky kind of happiness, but something much deeper, unshakable, profound. It's a kind of Happiness—Self-Realization—which I know helps not only one individual, but so many others.*

The huge sanctuary was ringed on three sides by galleries like the one we stood on, dominated at the far end by a flower-strewn stage hung with bright green sateen curtains. Above it paraded a garish collection of bas-relief images—painted Devis and Shivas, elephants, and monkeys. Bulking incongruously in front of this platform was a bank of electronic equipment, the familiar microphones, amplifiers, sound board, and speakers of the rock concert, here enlisted to swell the insistent, seductive beat of a dozen drums and sithars and harmoniums, and the enraptured voices of a thousand swaying bodies—Amma's devotees singing the evening *bhajans* or hymns.

At center stage, before a gleaming red and gold and silver altar adorned with an image of the goddess Devi, nearly eclipsed by the lush garlands and the hovering attendants and the blaring sound and the heat, a tiny, white-clad figure sat cross-legged, radiant, entranced. It was Mata Amritanandamayi, the Holy Mother, object and mirror of all this flamboyant ecstasy.

> *Mom, it's hard to accept, maybe, that one person meditating is helping the world, but I am positive that this is true.*

Facing the fantastic spectacle, I could not say if I was in the presence of a saint or had only stumbled onto the set of an Indiana Jones movie. Then, without warning, Jessica dropped to the floor and prostrated herself in the ancient and traditional posture of respect and adoration. I was overwhelmed, at once alienated, stunned, thrilled.

This single gesture, incarnating the unimaginable, embraced all my unspoken fears for my daughter. Yet as a traveler, I still relished the astonishing scene unfolding before me. As a human being, I felt myself most profoundly a mere voyeur, an outsider trapped within the puny grasp of my five senses. Incapacitated by culture and temperament, I was barred from entering into the humble, unquestioning devotion and rapture of spirit that formed the real spectacle here.

Chimgan

by Claudia J. Martin

"GET OFF THE bus and wait for further instructions. I will be back very soon." With those words, Kostya Muraviev exited the steamy interior of the school bus we had boarded hours earlier. It was well past midnight and we were somewhere in the middle of central Asia. By the cold light of the winter sky I watched Kostya turn the corner of an unlit building, garlanded with barbed wire, and disappear into the night. For a few moments I continued to hear his footsteps crunch in the frozen snow, the crisp sound growing fainter. Finally, I could hear nothing except the muted electric hum of a generator, and the rapid thump of my own heart.

It had not taken long for the rumor to spread among our group that Kostya was KGB. So no one dared to disobey the young guide who had met us at Sheremetievo airport in Moscow two days earlier, and whose good humor had increasingly faded the further we traveled from the Soviet capital. We stepped into the frozen Asian night, hastily pulling on hats and gloves, and flapping our arms against our bodies to try and stay warm. The driver quickly unloaded the bus. Then he drove away.

I wondered if the others were growing as anxious as I about this trip, but as the only woman on a twelve-"man" ski team, I decided it best not to voice my concern. My fellow travelers, mostly married men in their twenties and thirties, were the only people who, like me, had responded to an advertisement from an entity call Crosscurrents International, seeking participants for the first citizen-diplomat ski group to tour the various Soviet Republics. For $2,200 we would travel the width and breadth of the rapidly dissolving Soviet Union in three weeks, all meals, transport, and lodging included. But at this moment we were cold, hungry, exhausted, alone, and in the middle of Uzbekistan.

In front of us, beyond gates chained shut and topped with coils of barbed wire, I saw the silhouettes of several white buildings. There were no lights on except in one first floor window. Inside were two Soviet militiamen wearing great brown coats, fur hats, and semiautomatic rifles rakishly slung over their shoulders.

Suddenly, Kostya was inside talking with the militiamen. One guard accompanied Kostya outside and unlocked the gates, greeting us with a great, gold-toothed smile, and "PREEvet. PahZHAHloosta," while making a sweeping gesture towards the lit door.

"He says, 'Welcome to Chimgan,'" Kostya translated. We quickly gathered our luggage and skis and went indoors, grateful for some warmth.

Inside, the oversized lobby was dismal. Walls and floors were made of gray and brown pressed stone. Vinyl chairs in orange and avocado green were randomly strewn about the room. Two ancient pinball machines stood quietly in a corner. The room had a faintly acrid smell whose origin, I learned days later, was from the cats let loose at night to prowl the corridors for mice.

But still, it was the lobby of a ski resort: several pairs of beat-up Yugoslavian Mladlost skis leaned against one wall; bulletin boards held lists of schedules; children's drawings of skiers and mountains were strung across the staircase.

Kostya gave us our room assignments and told us the schedule we would keep for the next five days: the hours for meals, when and where to meet the bus to the ski area, that we could only shower between 7:00 and 8:00 in the morning and 6:00 and 7:30 in the evening, as that was when cold water was also sent through the pipes. Chimgan, built on natural hot springs, had plenty of heat and steaming hot water; it was cold water that was difficult to arrange, even in the middle of the winter.

"Russian engineering, Russian planning," Kostya advised us. We would receive this answer to many other questions in the days ahead.

The rooms were both austere and extravagant. Narrow cots had thick feather pillows. Gold floral wallpaper stopped six inches from the ceiling, as if they had run out and couldn't be bothered to get more. The bathrooms were made entirely of grimy brown tiles with a shower head in one wall and a drain in the middle of the floor, yet a beautiful gilt-framed mirror hung above the sink. I went to sleep wondering what had possessed me to travel twelve time zones to come to this place.

The next morning, after a breakfast of rice with flecks of meat, radishes, scallions, hard gray bread, pickled beets, soured goat cheese, and strong tea served in large painted bowls, we gathered our gear and paraded through the lobby, our day-glo ski clothes and state-of-the-art equipment drawing "oohs" and "aahs" from other vacationers. Kostya warned us to expect this: we were the first Westerners to stay here. On the bus we were given first choice of seats while a long line of Soviets waited: honored guests in this "classless society."

When we arrived at the base of the only chair lift, we found none of the expected facilities: no bathrooms, no lodge or food, only Uzbeki women with brightly colored head scarves selling roasted nuts. On the side of the lift shack there was a hand-painted map showing a single trail going straight down the vast expanse of peaks. We laughed at the absurd drawing and then took photos in front of it.

The chair lift stopped three-quarters up the mountain. Gear had to be hauled hundreds of yards uphill through deep snow to a small T-bar which took skiers to the top. When we asked Kostya why they hadn't ended the chair-lift closer to the T-bar he shrugged.

"Russian engineering, Russian planning." If we weren't so exhausted, we would have laughed.

At the top, we realized that, with all our fancy equipment, we were ill-prepared for Soviet skiing. There were no facilities and we had no food. Sensing our situation, we soon found ourselves adopted by the Soviets, by the Russians, Lithuanians, Ukrainians, Uzbeks, and dozens of other nationalities who shared their food and their thermoses of hot tea or cognac with us. In turn, we shared our ski equipment, electric socks, and portable cassette players with them. In the days to come they would share more: all-night dance parties at the ski pro's *dacha,* serious political discourses fueled by vodka and peppered with toasts of *mir* (peace) and *druzhba* (friendship), showings of bootlegged copies of James Bond movies, and clandestine trips to the border to watch the troops returning from Afghanistan.

At the end of that first day Kostya insisted that we board the return bus ahead of the long line of waiting Soviets, but we all shook our heads and refused; we would wait our turn. Kostya told us we were foolish, but as we rode back to the hotel, the Soviets serenaded us with "Yankee Doodle."

The First and Last Meal

by Carole L. Peccorini

I AM WAITING for my first evening meal in Borneo. I can see the black sky through chinks in the guest house roof, which explains why my mattress is slightly soggy. I learn later that the orangutans love to peel the shingles off the roof with a chomp and toss routine. It is 9:00 P.M. when the metal gong *brrrooooongs*. I slip on my flip-flops and join the other Earthwatch volunteers picking our way down the path toward the kitchen and dining enclosure. Our flashlight beams shift light from side to side, detecting puddles and gnarling roots, tangles of hanging vines, and finally a vast wave of fire ants crossing in front of us. We leap and duck, eager to reach the gentle glow of the kerosene lanterns and our dinner.

The stack of discarded shoes by the door grows. We snatch up our metal plates and a large oval spoon. As I head for a bench, I see that insects with white papery wings have also filled the room. Thousands are circling in a flight pattern, seemingly unorganized, but veering from any direct human hit.

"Flying termites," Professor Birute Galdikas announces, a hint of glee in her welcome. "A delicacy." I can't take my eyes off the opening and closing of her mouth. As she talks, winged termites swoop near the tide of her breath. "A cyclical event," she continues.

The jasmine rice is passed in a large metal bowl along with dark chard-like greens cooked in Indonesian spices, and small crisp fishes with eyes and fins intact.

"Pass the tea." Birute is smiling. Her eyes are warm. Three young orangutans are hanging on the screens, piqued with their own natural curiosity about human behavior. Their coppery hair stands two inches straight up on their heads and shoulders which gives them a look of constant surprise.

Suddenly, the flying termites begin to die. First one, two, three drop and rain down on our plates, the rice and fish, our tins of hot tea. The floor and tables are littered. The Dayak men and women grab several empty bowls and begin scooping them up. Mounds of winged carcasses are ceremonially carried to the kitchen to fry. We roll our eyes.

"Do you think they are actually going to serve us fried flying termites?"

Before this thought can be fully digested, an alert goes out. "Get your feet up, quick."

A full battalion of fire ants has come up through the floor boards and is swarming across the floor to harvest the dead termites for themselves. We hold our feet in the air. I snatch up my spoon and take another serving of rice and vegetables. My thigh and lower back muscles are quivering as the parade of bowls returns from the kitchen with piping hot and crunchy insects.

This was not included in the Professor's arrival lecture on the ten most likely ways you can die or get wounded in the rain forest. I had pictured dead wood falling 300 feet from the canopy and vipers that jump and leeches flipping end over end to attach themselves to my too-warm body for a blood meal. There are vibrant caterpillars that inflict intense pain, and plants that cause itching so fierce you want to tear your skin off with your own fingernails. And then the most disturbing warning of all....

"Orangutans rape women." We were told when you go into the forest wear long pants, long sleeves, and a hat. Don't speak above a whisper so the higher pitch of your voice will be disguised. Don't go out during your period. Carry a stick around camp, and always walk with another person.

We met Apollo Bob the day we arrived. Birute raised this abandoned baby orangutan at the camp and plans to return him to the rain forest as a young adult. Although orangutan youngsters would crawl into our arms to cuddle as a daily routine, she assured us that it is normal for an adolescent to have nothing but sex on his mind. Apollo Bob posted himself outside the guest house door.

"Don't even think about it, Apollo Bob," I warned each time he slowly turned his dark stare on me. "Don't you even think about it."

I survived three weeks without any dire calamities. I warded off leeches with Jungle Juice around the tops of my boots and along my shoelaces. I fell into a fetid swamp and bathed in the black water river. We witnessed the capture of a dragon-fish poacher who was put in charge of the evidence of his own crime according to Indonesian custom. And my yellow mesh T-shirt is now tie-dyed from being washed in buckets that did not include sorting dark from light.

Last meals are important rituals in Indonesia. There are speeches to make, gifts to wrap, foods to prepare. At last the gong clangs. At 10:00 P.M. we head out on a final trek down the trail of roots, puddles, and ants. My flashlight batteries are dead from the humidity and heat so I inch along the heels of the woman in front of me who still has a dim light. We carry gifts and are dressed in our cleanest clothes. I had stuffed a washable, emerald green, silk blouse in my pack at the last moment. I smooth out the wrinkles with my hand and put on my favorite earrings with faux gems that sparkle. We are going to a party. The damp forest is more familiar now. I jerk as a crash of branches breaks beside us in the dark and two feet grab my ankles. My heart whirls and plunges ahead, but my feet are stuck. Two long-haired arms wrap around my chest and across my back.

"Apollo Bob!" I shout. "Get off me!"

The women turn back to help, dropping the gifts in the dirt, and swat about Bob's head and back.

"Let go. Let go."

I tip into the mud. Apollo Bob holds fast. I squirm but cannot budge against the grip of his powerful arms and legs. My mind flashes to my silk blouse that he is pawing.

"Don't rip my blouse, don't you dare rip my good blouse, Apollo Bob."

Without warning, he flees.

I take a hand to regain an upright posture. My blouse seems intact. My last pair of clean khakis are filthy. I brush them off anyway. We gather up our gifts and resume our march toward dinner. More astonished than afraid, my mind begins to challenge that this fleeting encounter actually happened. As we enter the clearing around the dining hut, galloping feet race across the dirt. Someone shrieks, "It's Apollo Bob!" In a flash he clamps my legs in the vice of his grip, releases, turns, and charges into the forest again. The Dayak men leap from their benches inside the building but Apollo Bob is gone before they can get out the door. This times my knees are shaking.

"My God, did he actually single me out?"

That night we gave speeches. Birute translated from Indonesian to English and English to Indonesian. We ate and exchanged gifts and drank warm Coca Cola. At 1:00 A.M. we were dancing to the Dayak drums. The only sign that remained was two, long, muddy, hand prints on the back of my green silk blouse and a question in my mind about how I would tell my husband that I was jumped by an orangutan named Apollo Bob.

And There's the Rub

by Stacy Ritz

IF IT WASN'T for her tattooed forearms, mud encrusted finger-nails, clumsy 300-pound frame, and prevailing odor of street life, I wouldn't have minded her giving me a massage. As it was, I couldn't bear the thought of her touching me.

But what was I to say, confronted by this hulking vagabond of a woman who I had hired to rub my back? And what more could I expect from a far-flung outpost in Belize, where the sauna-like heat dulls the mind and the endless jungle becomes one's mental landscape. During the last few days, I had stared into the wild eyes of jaguars and stepped over man-sized boa constrictors as if they were fallen tree trunks on the forest floor. Surely I could escape from this sallow-faced, rheumy-eyed woman.

"I'm afraid I have a bad case of jellyfish stings," I said, stretching the neck of my T-shirt to reveal a cascade of red welts across my shoulders and chest. "Scuba diving, you know. The last thing I feel like having is a massage."

At that moment, in the dusty lobby of the motel where a sign enticed one to "Ease your tired body with a massage," the woman responsible for the sign puffed out her chest, contorted her craggy face and said: "Do you know how far I live? An hour away. I had to pay a taxi to get here, and you can't book out on me. We'll just work around those jellyfish bites."

I marveled at the ease with which she deflected rejection, a skill I would soon learn was but one of many in her grab bag of specialties. As I numbly followed her wide and wobbling body up the stairs to my cramped motel room, my mind rehearsed the fateful events that had brought me to this bizarre encounter:

Four months earlier, while researching a travel guidebook on Belize, I spied that inviting sign in the lobby of a small-town motel. Delirious from too much time in the jungle, I scribbled in my notebook that a massage would have been really nice. So several weeks before I was to depart for Belize again, I typed a short note to the motel: "Will be in town again on April 27. Can you talk to the masseuse and make sure she makes time for me?"

The motel did not respond, though when I checked in on April 27, the front desk clerk smiled wide, and announced in a most formal way that he would now introduce me to my masseuse. But when he led me to that ragtag woman oozing out of the lobby chair, I knew there was some mistake.

And now she was rubbing my shoulders. Or more like pummeling them. For her hands were not those of a potter who caressed his vessel into an ethereal pose; they were like the callused paws of a bricklayer who slapped and pounded materials into subjection. I complained twice that she was too rough, but her hands relented only a few seconds before resuming their furious work.

She had squeezed into a chair at the foot of the bed—her obesity did not allow her the luxury of standing for long periods—and I could feel her quick shallow breaths as she leaned across the side of my face. A ceiling fan barely circulated the oppressive heat, and the sheets beneath me got wet with sweat. The oil she kept squirting from a dirty ketchup bottle was grainy, and it felt like I was getting a scrubdown. I pictured Meryl Streep getting the radiation scoured off her in *Silkwood*.

Now, I have had many massages in many countries, and

none of them have lasted long enough, always leaving me wanting to continue the natural high that comes only from a massage. But this forty-five-minute massage refused to end, and I was certain the woman giving it would never go away. I trained my eyes on a piece of driftwood tacked to the wall so as not to glimpse her hair that was dull and matted, like the mane of a mare who had been rolling in the field, and her heavily creased face that bore the meanness of a prize fighter who had been knocked out one time too many.

Perhaps, in a way, she was a fighter, one of society's scrappers honed by days of hustling and nights of nowhere to sleep. She said she had come to Belize an unmemorable number of years ago from San Francisco, having thumbed her way across Mexico. She boasted of attending one of San Francisco's leading massage schools, and that she was also an expert in music and cooking and many other things I honestly do not remember. What I do recall is the relief I felt when she temporarily stopped pounding my neck to pull a cassette tape out of her crocheted purse.

No doubt, I thought, it is one of those "waves gently crashing and birds chirping" tapes I was accustomed to hearing during massages. At least now my mind could escape into the gentle sounds of nature. I waited for her to put on the tape, but instead she tossed it on the bed next to my head.

"Local *punta* rock, custom made by me," she said. "I know you want to buy one, so I'll just set it aside for you." I said nothing, but the throbbing, hard-driving sounds of *punta* rock began playing in my brain.

When she had finished, I pulled two Belizean twenties (equal to twenty U.S. dollars) from my backpack and handed it to her. Then she pushed the cassette in my hand and demanded another Belizean twenty. I pressed the tape back into her hand and told her I could not buy it, but again she handed it back to me, then I to her. And suddenly we seemed like two Mayan warriors dueling in a game whose complexities went far beyond the wood-paneled walls of this tiny motel room.

Don't ask me how, but I finally won out. I remember pointing to the door, and after I heard it slam I lay back on the sweat-soaked bed and fixated on the churning ceiling fan, my sore, stinking body decompensating, like Martin Sheen in *Apocalypse Now,* spread-eagle on his bed and enveloped by the stench of battle.

But my battle was over, and all that remained was a bruised body and psyche. I reached into my backpack, pulled out a bottle of Caribbean White Rum, and started on the path to recovery.

Sahafin Americani

by Larry Collins

To a young Middle Eastern correspondent for the United Press, 7:00 A.M. was a sacred hour. No matter how much alcohol might be befuddling my brain, as soon as the alarm sounded my hand would shoot up from under the covers and punch on my transistor to the BBC's World News Roundup—the best way to learn if something had happened the evening before in the far-flung parish where the UP had assigned me.

Something had on that March morning in 1959. In the northern Iraqi town of Mosul, the BBC revealed, a group of army officers had seized power and were challenging the Moscow inspired regime of Brigadier General Karim Abdul Kassem. I was out of bed in a second. How was I to get to Mosul before anybody else? A worldwide scoop! Glory! A Pulitzer Prize! Maybe even more money—although with the UP that was unlikely. My first call revealed that the Baghdad airport was closed to incoming traffic. Natch. That was the reflex gesture of menaced regimes.

There had to be another way to get in. Patience, counseled my older, wiser colleagues. Eventually, the Iraqis will open the airport and we'll all fly in together.

Patience wouldn't get me a worldwide scoop. I picked up my freelance photographer, Paul Davis, and a Palestinian pal, Said Abou Rish, who strung for the *London Daily Mail*. We would certainly need his Arabic along the way. We headed over the mountains by taxi to Damascus to catch a flight from Damascus via Aleppo to Al Qamishli in the northeastern corner of Syria, nestled up against the Iraqi frontier. Syria's United Arab Republic government of the day detested the anti-Nasserite Kassem. They were probably involved in the coup. Once we got there, you could bet they'd run us into Mosul to record the heroic struggle against the tyrant in Baghdad.

Normally, the Syrian border guards greeted American journalists—*Sahafin Americani*—with about as much warmth as a polecat greets an intruder on his turf, but that morning they whisked us right through and we made our flight with minutes to spare. I looked around. Not a single fellow journalist on the plane! We were off to our scoop.

Now there was one minor problem. Al Qamishli was in a restricted military zone. But we'd talk our way around that one when the time came, we were sure. We landed in Aleppo to take on a few more passengers. Paul and I huddled in our seats, looking at our shoes trying to be as inconspicuous as possible. The door closed. The engines sparked. We were off!

No, we weren't. The engines stopped. The door opened. A man in uniform came up the aisle looking for the "Sahafin Americani."

We explained our sacred mission to tell the world of the heroic struggle of his brave Iraqi brothers to free themselves from the grips of the tyrant of Baghdad, blah, blah, blah ...

He wasn't buying.

Where was his boss? I asked. Maybe we'd find more comprehension higher up the bureaucratic ladder.

It was Ramadan. He was home in bed. Off the plane, was the reply.

So in the office we waited for the boss to get to work hoping for a later plane. Finally, he arrived, wrapped in that vile humor one often finds in the Middle East during the fasting month of Ramadan. Paul made the mistake of lighting a cigarette, a forbidden act for the devout during daylight in that month. His gesture did not endear him to the officer, who informed us under no circumstances were we going to the restricted zone.

Said suggested we rent a cab, drive across the frontier to Adana, Turkey, and there rent another car and driver to take us along Turkey's southern border to Mardin, only a few miles from the land crossing between Turkey and Syria, and just outside Al Qamishli. Off we went.

Getting into Adana was easy but once there we prowled the main square looking for someone ready to drive us to Mardin. Despite the promise of a flow of dollars, our proposition did not elicit many takers. Finally, a gentleman, no more than five-foot-two, wearing a tattered overcoat over pajamas and a blue and white knit skull cap said he'd do it for five hundred American (dollars). That was a bit steep for my penny pinching employers, but what's five hundred bucks measured against a great worldwide scoop?

His car, a 1948 ex-U.S. Air Force Chevrolet which had clearly already done far more than its share of miles in its service to the nation, was going to have to do about four hundred more. Could it?

"No problem," the driver, Abdullah, assured us.

"Gas along the way?"

"No problem."

"Accommodations for the night if necessary?"

"No problem."

As it turned out those were the answers we got because they were about the only words Abdullah could speak in English. Off we went.

Eighty miles out of Adana, our pot-holed macadam two

lane black top turned to—a super highway?

No, a dirt track. Now one does not make great time on a dirt track, particularly when 1) it's full of stones which are not particularly tender on tires that are 2) as slick as a satin bow. Every fifty miles or so, we could count on a flat. Abdullah had thoughtfully stocked the trunk with two extra spare wheels. Around midnight we arrived in the charming little town of Urfa.

We booked into the local five-star hotel, the only cara-vansary in town as it happened. The rooms were the size of a large closet. The beds were Indian rope charpoy style—great for bad backs. But it was the plumbing system that was the most captivating aspect of the place. The clientele was all male and the "rooms" were arranged in a long line on one floor. At the rear of each was a "V" shaped trough which ran at a de-scending angle along the entire line of rooms. A trickle of water ran through it and the guests were invited, in case of need, to contribute to that water flow. I dozed off to the symphony of over-full Turkish bladders splashing out the evening's harvest into the trough a few doors upstream from my room.

The good news, off the BBC the next morning, was that Baghdad airport was still closed. The worldwide scoop was still ours! Off to Al Qamishli. We got to Mardin, only twenty miles from the frontier and decided to visit the post office to send London a cable advising them of our whereabouts. As we came out a chap in civilian clothes came up to us.

"Turkish Intelligence," he said. "Your papers."

We were in a restricted military zone, he explained, and as a consequence we were under arrest.

But we were NATO allies, friends of the great and heroic Turkish people, the heroes of Korea, blah, blah, blah.... No good. We were under arrest. Finally we persuaded him to escort us under armed guard down to the Syrian frontier and hurl us across the border into the Arab netherlands.

By the time we got to the frontier, however, it was closed for the day. No one had crossed over here, the frontier guard explained, for six months. So another night in Turkey. This time we were accommodated in a stable.

At eight the next day, again reassured by the BBC that Baghdad was still closed, we were ready to haul our bags over the half mile of no man's land to Syria. There was at the time—and is today—little love lost between the Turks and their southern neighbors so it was not a warm and open crossing point.

"Watch out for the mines," the Turkish guard called out as we left.

"Where?" I asked.

"Who knows?" was the answer.

At first, the dumbfounded Syrian border guards didn't know what to do with us. They had never seen Americans of any sort crossing there, let alone Sahafin. They were about to let us go when cooler heads prevailed. They arrested us.

Said, as it turned out, had Palestinian cousins living there. We convinced the guard to take us to their home while we tried to straighten things out. The cousins explained that, sure, the uprising had been inspired in part by Syria, that they were running arms over the frontier to Mosul, and in all probability they could run us in with them. There it was. The worldwide scoop, the Pulitzer.

While we savored that prospect, a Syrian major showed up and disabused us of our notions. We were still under arrest and were being deported—back to Turkey. At noon we trudged back across the frontier. The Syrians did not warn us about mines. The Turks, were surprised to see us, although not so surprised that they didn't arrest us again. Two soldiers were detailed to take us by bus back to Mardin. There, by chance, we stumbled into Abdullah. A ride back to Adana?

No problem. Five hundred American.

It was back in Adana the next morning that the BBC informed us the revolt was over. The first Middle East Airlines flight full of journalists had just arrived in the Iraqi capital.

Adrift

by Joe Cummings

"G'DAY MATE!" I opened my eyes and looked up from my sling chair. It had been a hard morning's work canvassing the Carita area for an update of Lonely Planet's Indonesia guidebook, and I was enjoying a brief rest on the beach. The Australian standing over me in denim cutoffs, shoulder length, dirty blonde hair, and a muscled, sun-reddened chest didn't wait for a counter-greeting. "A few of us are hiring a boat to have a look at Crack-a-toe. Tomorrow morning, around five thirty. Four hours out, four hours back. Wanna come along?"

I didn't want to rise that early and I really needed to be moving along to the next area on my itinerary, West Java's Badui region. Fascinated by stories of mysterious priests who never left Badui Dalam—a zone at the center of Badui that was off limits to all outsiders, I hoped to grab a peek into the heart of this little known area. The Sundanese claimed that the clairvoyant Badui priests instantly knew when anyone intended to breach the invisible line between Outer and Inner Badui. If they sensed the threat was real, these priests could conjure a powerful hex that would cause debilitating illness, even death, to the potential interloper.

But this was an opportunity to see Krakatau, site of the largest volcano eruption in human history. I had talked to the German owner of the backpacker's resort where I was staying and he had said the only boats to Krakatau were those chartered from the Indonesian park service post farther south in Labuhan. The going rate for the 100-kilometer round trip over

118

the Straits of Sunda was 800,000 rupiah (around 400 dollars at the time). I wasn't willing to spend that much on an extinct volcano.

When questioned about his arrangements, the Aussie said he'd found a cheaper local alternative—a fishing boat whose owner was willing to take a group of around ten paying passengers for a total of 200,000 rupiah. That would work out to about ten dollars each if they could fill the boat. Briefly weighing the loss of one day against the opportunity to observe and photograph Krakatau at such an affordable price, I decided Badui could wait.

~

It was difficult to abandon the comfortable palm-thatched bungalow at 5:30 A.M. Three Sundanese *nelayan* (fishermen) and a brilliant sunrise greeted our group of ten at the beach. As I rolled up my trouser legs to wade out to the wooden, African Queen-style boat, the Aussie chided me for being so fastidious.

"What's the matter, mate, afraid to get your pants wet?"

Once we left the protection of Carita Bay, the boat's small gas engine strained against the chop. About five hours out, the engine sputtered to a halt but the crew got it going again within ten minutes. The promised four-hour crossing to Krakatau took six and a half hours, but the remnants of Krakatau's great crater rim were impressive.

Carpeted with tropical scrub, the green, crescent-shaped islands surrounded a new cinder cone that had risen since the volcano's nineteenth-century eruption. The Javanese called the new cone Anak Krakatau, "Child of Krakatau." Thin curls of smoke issued from vents in the cone's black, granulated surface. Sulfurous lava leaked from one side of the cone into the sea, sending billowing spirals of white steam skyward. We produced the appropriate gestures of awe, snapped photographs, and hiked to the cone's summit for lunch.

Because the outbound voyage had taken so long, the fishermen were anxious for us to leave after only forty-five minutes. The sky was clouding over as we reboarded the boat, and a general nervousness set in. We were a couple of hours east of Krakatau when the storm began to blow and the engine failed again. This time the crew wasn't able to bring the engine back to life. As the sun dropped over the horizon, we drifted southwest with the current, away from Java and the rest of Indonesia.

∾

Another ten-footer slapped against the side, washed over the deck, and the same cold equation came forth. The boat shuddered on impact, lifted with the swell, and teetered on the edge of a watery void as I clung to the stripped mast to avoid slipping over the bow.

When smaller swells buffeted the powerless craft, I tried to ride the deck as if it were an oversized surfboard, flexing my knees with the bumps to avoid being thrown into the sea.

For some it was quite a struggle. They retched and pinched their faces; if I could have heard anything above the *musique concrete* of wind and sea, I imagined a tremendous tearing, scouring, gargling sound.

A Scotch traveler balanced on the foredeck next to me. We had occupied that spot since just before sunset, when the big swells were making trouble but before the storm had arrived in earnest. We shared this belief: The reason every one of our boat-mates—including the Sundanese crew of three—was sick was that they hadn't fixed their minds on the horizon after the first sign of rough seas. I had experienced the hell of pro-tracted seasickness much earlier in my travel career, and I wasn't going to allow a reprise.

So the Scot and I stood there on the deck, with our hands clutching the low cabin roof for stability, while focusing on the fading rays of the sun setting over Krakatau. In between intentionally distracting chat about the malt whiskeys of Scot-land, the ashrams of India, and whatever other compost trav-elers like to churn, we vowed to hold the image of that reddish horizon in our minds even after it wasn't visible to the eye.

After a while, as the larger waves crashed over the deck at five-minute intervals, the salt water began to sting sharply through my soaked clothing. And by midnight, with high winds and no prolonged relief between apartment-sized waves, we felt the cold deeply. Sitting in the cramped, open-sided, vomit-and-sea-washed cabin was no relief, especially since, in that four-foot-high space, I couldn't flex with the surf or focus on the imaginary line where sky meets sea.

From time to time I tried to rouse a slight Englishman in baggy shorts, punk haircut, and wire-rim glasses from his sin-gle-minded posture, which hadn't varied one inch since I'd seen him unfurl his own liquid banner several hours earlier. He sat on one of the parallel cabin benches with his upper torso stretched flat across his thighs, arms folded around his knees as the waves washed through the cabin around him and his companions writhed and grimaced, puked and howled.

"You're going to destroy your back sitting doubled over like that for so long," I tried to admonish him. He twisted his head to the side just long enough to utter what I imagined to be a Cockney curse, lost in the wind.

$\sim$

Around 3:00 A.M. the swells deepened yet again and the Sundanese still couldn't get the engine going. The oldest of the three prostrated himself in the engine hold and began murmuring prayers to Allah. Looking into his eyes, I could see he reckoned Judgment Day had arrived.

Earlier in the night our Australian patron had used every epithet in his vocabulary to curse the Sundanese crew for the engine failure. Now he was shaking vigorously with cold—in just a tank top and shorts—and alternating between gasping sobs and bursts of laughter. The Scot, his Swiss girlfriend, and I pulled the Aussie into the low cabin, wrapped him in Javanese sarongs, and formed a tight circle around him in an attempt to warm his body and calm his hysteria.

The ordeal came to an end after the sun rose the next day and the storm abated. The Sundanese were able to dismantle and rebuild the engine using nothing more than a hammer and chisel, replacing a blown gasket with some hastily tooled leather scraps. Twenty-six hours after we had departed Carita Beach, the boat found its home mooring. Celebrating what seemed a shared miracle, we hugged each other, and kissed the sand.

$\sim$

I never made it to Inner Badui, having decided that the secrets of the priests might best be left out of guidebooks.

The Flight from Hell

by Donald W. George

THE NICE THING about traveling by airplane is that you're stuck. Not only is there nowhere to go, there's also nothing immediate to worry about (unless, of course, you're one of those people who worries with each air pocket leap that the plane is about to plunge you and every other living soul around you into a nightmarish, flaming death—an obsession from which I happily have never suffered).

In short: You have to relinquish control.

Ahead of you stretches two or six or however many hours of uninterrupted indulgence. If you want a drink or a snack, you push a button.

Otherwise, you are purely, blissfully, on your own.

You can snooze. You can daydream. You can write in your journal, or read the novel that has been lying by your bed for months.

You can concoct elaborate fantasies, delve deep into memory, or trace a coherent, connected string of thoughts the way mundane life never lets you.

No phone interruptions. No knocks on the door. No E-mail messages.

Your captivity is your liberation.

And strange and wonderful things can happen on airplanes. On my first solo trip abroad, when I was a college junior going to Paris to live for the summer, I was seated next to a female student who serendipitously enough was doing the same thing. We ended up going to the *Comedie Française*, exploring smoky sawdust restaurants and walking long nights along the Seine together.

A few years later, when I was flying to Tokyo to start a two-year teaching fellowship and was full of fears about that vastly unknown land, I sat next to a young woman who had been living in Kyoto for two years—and who, by the end of the journey, had answered my hungry questions and allayed my ignorant fears.

Alas, not all airplane trips are quite so happy. Like most travelers, I have endured my share of drinks spilled in my lap, babies wailing in my ear and enthusiastic chatterers chattering endlessly through a trans-Atlantic night. I even came close to losing my life one youthful summer when a grinning Tanzanian pilot decided to show me just how close his two-seat propeller plane could come to the waters off the coast of Zanzibar.

And then there was the journey that I fondly think of as "The flight from hell." This was not an adventure of the life-threatening kind. But it is one of those surreal vignettes I have come to cherish as examples of the fundamental lunacy of the traveler's life.

Here is that tale:

San Francisco International Airport, January 6, 11:12 P.M.— I just flew in from Jamaica, and boy, are my arms tired.

Not just my arms, actually, but my legs, my head, and my heart are tired too. Let me explain why.

My wife, daughter, and I had just spent a long, slow, eminently relaxing week in Jamaica and were at the airport in Montego Bay waiting for the 10:15 Air Jamaica flight to San Francisco via Los Angeles.

There were a few minor irritations to begin with—the plane boarded a half-hour late, then flew across the island for twenty minutes, and landed in Kingston to take passengers (a stop the airline makes only on its Saturday flights, something we had overlooked), and so we had to wait another hour before taking off again.

Once we were winging through that bright blue Caribbean sky toward Los Angeles all was well—until we landed in Los Angeles, that is, when something extraordinary happened.

I have never heard of this happening before, and veteran travelers I have since checked with had never heard of it either.

But first, a little background: The flight was an Air Jamaica flight, but since Air Jamaica does not have enough planes to cover the route, it had subcontracted with Hawaiian Air to provide the actual service. This meant that the plane's logo said Hawaiian Air, the flight attendants were in Hawaiian Air aloha shirts, and incongruous ukulele music greeted us when boarding in Montego Bay.

It also meant that the ensuing demi-disaster was the responsibility of Hawaiian Air.

This is what happened, or at least, this is what various airline workers told me happened: The co-pilot on the Montego Bay-Los Angeles run was scheduled to be replaced with a fresh co-pilot when the plane landed in Los Angeles. During the course of the flight, however, someone in Central Scheduling changed his/her mind and decided that the co-pilot should stay in the cockpit all the way to San Francisco.

Unfortunately, no one told the co-pilot.

So we landed in Los Angeles, and while the Los Angeles bound passengers were grabbing their carry-on bags and disembarking from the plane, the co-pilot was hustling off too, bound (I imagine) for his car and a long, slow, well-deserved drive into the sunset.

They got off; we stayed on. And sat.

And sat.

The first onboard person to realize what had happened was the pilot, who dashed off the plane to try to catch up with the co-pilot, but it was too late. There followed a frantic scrambling by Hawaiian Air officials to locate that co-pilot or any co-pilot who could accompany the plane to San Francisco.

After we had been on the ground for about a half-hour with no apparent movement of any sort, tension began to creep through the plane. A few passengers asked what was going on, but the flight attendants—who knew more than they were telling, I think, but perhaps didn't know the whole story—would only say they didn't know. When I pressed one, he told me that the pilot had gotten off the plane and that perhaps there was some sort of mechanical difficulty he wanted the maintenance people to look into.

And so we sat. And no announcement was made. No food was available—it had already been unloaded. After forty-five minutes someone realized there were beverages still stocked onboard and the flight attendants began serving those to passengers who asked.

As it became clear that something untoward was delaying us, passengers who had connecting flights in San Francisco began to ask if they could get off the plane to make other arrangements. Some passengers asked if food could be brought onboard, or if they could at least walk into the terminal to stretch their legs. But no San Francisco-bound passengers were allowed to disembark because they were supposed to clear customs in San Francisco, and no food was authorized to be brought on.

And so we waited, tired, hungry, and irritated.

After ninety minutes, the silence had become mutinous. Then the pilot came on the intercom to announce that the first officer had left the plane because he wasn't informed about the scheduling change, and that the airline was looking for him or for a replacement, and that we would be kept informed about the situation. He apologized, perfunctorily I thought, for the inconvenience.

After another half-hour he announced that a new flight had been arranged for us, and that all San Francisco-bound passengers were to get off the plane, go through customs in Los Angeles, pick up new tickets from the Air Jamaica agent, and proceed to the USAir gateway for the flight to San Francisco.

Customs at LAX was in chaos. The lines snaked interminably, and our unexpected presence added a few hissing coils.

It was then that I decided to keep this log of ensuing events:

> 8:48 P.M. (This was Jamaica time—our body time and my watch time; it was 5:48 P.M. West Coast time.) We have cleared customs and are waiting for our baggage to appear.

After we get our baggage, the Air Jamaica agent gives us vouchers for the 7:00 P.M. USAir flight and tells us to follow her. I drag our bags through a terminal scene out of a science fiction movie—you know, the moment when the monster's first been seen and a million people are trying to flee through a single doorway.

We stop at an area where steaming passengers are waiting to find out what's going on. Our Air Jamaica baggage tickets are hastily ripped off and replaced with handwritten stickers bearing a USAir flight number. We pray they will reach San Francisco with us.

We are told we don't need confirmed seats for the USAir flight, but should simply exit the terminal, look for a green and white

"A" bus to take us to the USAir terminal, and proceed to the gateway, where we should explain to the USAir ticket agents that we are from the Air Jamaica flight.

9:48 We go to the USAir ticket agents and explain that we are from the Air Jamaica flight and they say since we don't have confirmed seats we will be put on standby. We tell them we were told we didn't need confirmed seats. They ask who told us that. We say the Air Jamaica agent. They say she had no authority to tell you that. We say we don't care, we want to get seats for the flight. They say sorry, but we can't guarantee that because you don't have confirmed seats.

Now, waiting standby, I notice that the flight we hope to take is number 2777, whereas the flight number written on our luggage tags is 2017—sayonara, suitcases.

We have not had anything to eat since we were somewhere over the Caribbean in another life.

10:02 After some tense standby moments, our names are called for the 7:00 P.M. flight.

11:12 We land in San Francisco after a smooth flight—even sandwiches were served.

11:42 We are waiting for our luggage.

11:52 The carousel is moving and luggage is tumbling onto it like manna from heaven. And there are our bags. Ah, deliverance.

12:06 Well, demi-deliverance. We are missing one piece, which the USAir agent assures me will be on the next flight, which is due to arrive in ten minutes. Our three-year-old daughter, who has burst into tears only twice during this entire ordeal—remarkable restraint, it seems to me—has fallen asleep on the carpet and we decide to wait.

I approach another father from the same flight and say, "So what do you think?" He says, "I think Hawaiian Air owes us a nice dinner in Waikiki."

We mull this over for a few minutes. He looks at my scribbled notes, then at me. "The flight from hell," he says.

Ai Yi

by Molly Giles

OF ALL THE things in my backpack, the thing I hated most was the canvas air mattress. It took up too much space, wouldn't fold flat, and weighed more than my jeans, hiking boots, and guidebooks combined. Plus it was useless: Ken and I had been in Baja a week and hadn't camped yet. We'd spent every night either in a palapa or a cheap hotel. Several times I'd been tempted to ditch it—I thought of "forgetting" it on the bus in Todos Santos or on the bone strewn beaches of Puerto Aquaverde. The morning we were to leave La Paz I picked it up and looked longingly at the air shaft out our hotel window. But Ken had already packed his, along with the camp stove, tent, fishing pole, and frying pan we hadn't used either, so once again I stuffed the stiff green thing into my bag, hoisted the bag onto my back, and lumbered downstairs to the street.

The taxi driver grunted sympathetically as he dropped the pack into his trunk and he grunted again when Ken and I told him we were going to the harbor to catch the ferry for the thirteen-hour voyage across the Sea of Cortez to Topolobampo.

"He wants to know," Ken said, turning to me with a smile, "where we're going to sleep." I smiled back. We were going to splurge. We had made arrangements to sleep in a private state-room with a porthole from which we could watch the sun set and rise as porpoises played in our wake.

Four hours later we sat in a low-ceilinged, hot, dark, airless hold with a hundred other people. After waiting in line at the ticket office, we found out that our "arrangements" meant nothing; this ferry had no staterooms. What it did have were two cramped seats in a crooked row separated from other rows by a narrow aisle. Babies screamed on all sides of us. Chickens squawked from crates shoved under the seats. A group of cowboys sat in the back, drinking beer, and singing. Madonna keened from a teenager's radio. The latrine, already over-flowing, added its odors to the hot press of packed bodies.

Colorful, we decided, and no worse than being on a bus, really, except that most of the buses we'd been on had been moving. This boat wasn't moving. Ken began talking with an old fisherman who was traveling to Los Mochis to see his son.

"He says we ought to stake a space on the aisle," Ken said. "That's where people sleep." I looked and saw the aisle was, indeed, filling up fast with people sitting or already lying down.

"You know what would come in handy here?" Ken patted his back. "Our gear. Let's blow those mattresses up."

We did, overlapping them on the floor, and found we were sandwiched without an inch to spare between a family of six and a family of ten. Ken settled in, knees drawn up, hands crossed behind his head.

"Just what I've always wanted," he said. "Nothing to do but lie back on a big boat and relax."

Just then a door opened somewhere and we got a whiff of fresh air, followed by an equally welcome whiff of hot food. People began to line up at a makeshift lunch counter and I soon joined them, returning with two paper plates of chicken and beans and sweet white bread. It was unnerving picking my way over the bodies strewn in the aisle, stepping over wide-eyed babies and wary grandmothers, curled in their shawls, and I repeated "Pardon" as I walked back to the mattresses. Ken and I ate hungrily and grinned as the boat, with a bellow, started moving at last.

The movement, however, was straight up and down. Had a storm blown up while we'd been locked inside? We looked at the old fisherman. He was clutching a crucifix. Uh oh, we thought. After three minutes of up and down the boat suddenly rolled to the right and held there. After a long second it straightened and lunged to the left. Everyone on board was silent. Then a baby began to vomit.

"Ai yi," a woman said quietly from the back. "Ai yi," another answered from the front. We heard them both choke and vomit. "Ai yi," came from the family behind us. "Ai yi," chorused the family in front of us. From the cowboys: "Ai yi," from the fisherman: "Ai yi," from grandmothers, businessmen, children, and priests: "Ai yi." Ken and I hugged our knees and tried not to listen. When we saw a thick river of vomit moving toward us on the floor, we tried not to look. We tried not to smell, not to touch, not to speak. There was nothing to say anyway, except "Ai yi"—and we did not want to say that.

We were the only people on the boat who did not get sick that night. Our air-filled canvas mattresses cushioned the heaves of the waves and repelled the waves of heaves all around us. We stayed high and dry. Around midnight the wind dropped, the sea calmed, and everyone slept. At sunrise, I opened my eyes, and made my way through the wreckage to the *Damas*. It was unenterable, the floor afloat in sewage. I edged toward the deck for air. An elegant young man, leaning on the railing, beckoned to me and said in English, "Look." I followed his finger to a swirl of black fins in the water below: sharks. I staggered back inside. Ken was already packing; he had deflated his mattress and was folding it into a big plastic bag. I picked mine up by one corner. It was drenched, rancid, dripping. I caught the eye of a pregnant Indian woman about my age who was nursing one baby and braiding the hair of another; she held my gaze and shook her head slightly. I nodded. Enough was enough. I kept my head low and slid my mattress over the slick filthy floor with my foot to a corner by an overflowing garbage can.

"Gracias," I said to it, "and adios."

Rafting the Sewers of the Rhineland

by Louis B. Jones

My friend Tim and I were in Salzburg's Altstadt leaning on the railing of a bridge over the Salzach River watching the water flow beneath us. Our belongings were on the pavement beside us. We had just left Die Blaue Gans, our cheap hotel, where we couldn't afford to pay the bill anymore, and were trying to figure out what to do with the little money we had left.

There was a sporting goods store in sight where an orange inflatable rubber boat hung in the window. Its price was 600 schillings, or twenty-some U.S. dollars. I persuaded Tim— who was initially skeptical—that this boat could carry us along the swift smooth currents of the Salzach River, which on the map debouched into ... the Rhine? The Rhine—or else the Seine, I forget, we were sixteen years old—*some* concatenation of rivers would carry us to the blue waters of the Atlantic Ocean. And from there, I promised, the whole of Europe would be open to us. We could float southward along balmy coasts, pushing away from the beaches, until we reached the sunny decadent places. We had just spent some days in London sleeping in Hyde Park in steady rains, sheltering in the Underground; and a dampness pervaded our bones which we now wanted to dry out.

So we did it. We bought the boat; and we bought an immense, hard sausage with a paper ring labeling it "Braunegertof," and a bottle of resinous Tafelwein, and some hard bread. In case of rain, we could always sleep under the overturned boat on the bank. Our new boat was canoe-shaped, two big inflated wieners of Day-Glo orange rubber united at both ends, with inflated ribs running along its floor. A gusset of rubber on its bow bore the emblem of a teddy bear, along with the brand name "Sevylor." It came with two paddles, as tall as we were, of varnished blonde hardwood.

The sky was blue and clear. Under that same bridge on a cobbled shore, we put the boat in the water—the salesman in the sporting goods store had unpinned the display boat from the window for us, so we didn't have any initial inflating to do—and we threw in our belongings. I took the stern position because, having been a Boy Scout, I had learned the feather-stroke and the J-stroke at Camp Ma-Ka-Ja-Wan, and would therefore be the better pilot. As we drifted out of the old city, the river took a gradual long bend to the right and then, after a quarter of a mile, a long bend to the left. We began to move out into open country, where fat cows grazed on hillsides and castles glistened on high bluffs, exactly as I had pictured. Germany was on one side, Austria on the other.

I said, "This is fine."

"Yes," said Tim. "This is good. Not like London."

"No, London wasn't good."

"But this is fine," said Tim. "This is the best."

We weren't daunted by the first stretch of whitewater rapids we came to. The boat picked up speed and we swept past little submerged boulders. At this rate, we would enter Paris any day!

At a bend in the river, a bad smell arose, and, in a black cloud of flies, a rusty old crane lifted animal carcasses from a dump truck into a rust-freckled, open vent in the roof of a brick building. It was a sausage factory, surmounted by a sign displaying the name "Braunegertof." We rummaged through our packs to find it and threw our big Wurst overboard, where it sank, and for a few miles we told each other that there was nothing unusually sordid about Braunegertof in particular, that all sausage is manufactured under such conditions.

Soon that first morning, we had our first capsize. Whitewater river rafting wasn't a widely popular sport then (this was twenty-five years ago), and Tim and I thought we had discovered something strange and intimate and peculiar. We looked forward to every bumpy part, staving off rocks with our paddles. But eventually we tipped, and we had to chase along the riverbank retrieving our snagged belongings. Those that sank, we dived repeatedly for. We spread everything on a rock in the sun, and that night camped there. The next day we made good progress, capsizing every few miles, until the river widened and flattened. The heat and mosquitoes rose around us, and we had to start paddling. It was hard work. The river was more like a lake now. A light rain had begun falling in the summer heat, and as we paddled we wore rubber ponchos which trapped our bodies' humidity. The smell from the water wasn't very good. We were coming into a city, and the effluent kept smelling worse. The lake kept getting wider and glassier. Soon we heard the steady thunder ahead. A concrete precipice spilled the river over a drop of I-don't-know-how-many feet.

We were able to paddle—fast—to shore: a vertical concrete shore where rusty iron rungs, like big staples, provided a way up. It was tough—it was touch and go—dragging the boat up that ten-foot wall. The water's surface sucked on the underside of the boat. But we did it. We kept the boat. (Later in London we stuffed it in a train-station locker; but the paddles of course wouldn't fit. So, as we walked around town looking for a legendary nightclub, The Rainbow, where the early

Yardbirds and the early Stones and *everybody* had casually jammed, we were stopped by a London cop with the ancient query: "What's all this then?" carrying our immense paddles at night through civilized London like visiting Watusi.) Anyway, with a lot of sweaty effort in the German rain, we saved our rubber boat from the Salzach River.

In the little town of Braunau, we emerged dripping from the sewage canal, and people edged away from us. We had come up in the center of a commercial district where, in a small kiosk, a man sold *heisse Wurstchen* on flimsy paper plates with a dab of brown mustard on the rim. We sat on the railing of the canal beside our Day-Glo boat and ate, hungrily, these sausages whose skins were tough and balloon-like, hardly to be punctured under grinding incisors. At that moment we were so completely happy that it's surely wrong to include this story in a collection titled *I Should Have Stayed Home.*

A Tourist in Haiti

by Larry O'Connor

FROM THE HOTEL balcony I can see the pool. It's wide and whitewashed with metal frames of chaise lounges arranged in the sun on the far side. The shady poolside bar sits unattended, and I can see, if I crane my neck, that there's not a single bottle of booze behind it. The lounge frames are flecked in rust.

Dr. Philipot, a character in Graham Greene's novel, *The Comedians,* died in this pool. And from his suite at poolside the cartoonist Charles Addams drew the twisted spires and hemorrhoidal doodads of this most gingerbread of places, the Hotel Oloffson. There are other places to stay in Haiti, but none in Port-au-Prince with such history—and secure gates to keep beggars and thieves out.

Beyond the sweet-smelling lane of bougainvillaea and mango trees, stands the six-foot wall topped with razor wire and the new wrought-iron gates. The manager of the Oloffson says the gates came in a dream. A peasant saw in a vision the great black liberator, Jean-Jacques Dessalines, in a plume hat and shiny tunic on a black stallion.

"Go to the city and have a gate erected at the hotel," the ghost of Dessalines declared. The peasant then made his pilgrimage to the hotel, and the manager, no scoffer at visions, had a foundry pour the molds that afternoon. The gates were up by the end of the week.

I've decided not to fool with visions either, and have vowed to remain behind the gates until my departure date. I had planned to stay in Haiti for ten days for the travel guide com-

pany I work for, but I changed my ticket and am leaving tomorrow, three days early. For half my stay I've been holed up here,
reading *The Comedians* and doodling in a journal, taking to
heart a line from the guide I'm updating: "Indeed it's possible to spend the rest of your time basking and relaxing and
forgetting that the world outside exists." It's one of the few
lines I'm not thinking of rewriting.

The work has not gone well. It's almost impossible to get
through to hotel owners and restaurateurs: telephone lines
constantly go dead; taxis get caught in hours-long traffic jams.
Nobody goes out at night. At sundown, journalists, mission
workers, and other fun seeking hotel guests all converge at the
Oloffson bar because of the curfew. So the last few nights I've
taken my lists of hotels and restaurants into the bar. The first
night two English travel agents hopped like country rabbits
about the low-slung wicker seats and glass tables, snapping
photos of Trevor, the curly-haired journalist from the *Guardian*
and his entourage of fresh-faced admirers, while mission workers from Barbados, St. Martinique, and Pittsburgh sipped
frosted drinks, grumbling of their supervisors. One night it
seemed every other person was a restaurateur or an employee
of the ministry of tourism, so I got some work done.

"What became of the Pétionville espresso bar that opened
in 1989?" I asked. "Does it still take American Express? Has
the adjoining fitness club kept its discount rates on Thurs-
days?"

The next day I changed my ticket. I'd like to write more in
my journal, but I'm finding it hard to keep my eyes open. For
almost a week now I've slept very little. A man no one ever
sees stays in his room twenty-four hours a day, with CNN blaring at top volume. ("CRITICS SAY, PURE COUNTRY IS PURE
GOLD" … "HAVE YOU DRIVEN A FORD, LATELY?") It's said

he's the only one in the hotel who hasn't cut a deal with the manager and is paying full price, so he can do as he pleases. If not for the empty bottles of Guinness and half-eaten, white-bread sandwiches on a china dish that appear every day, I'd think the room had in it only a television. It's less distracting being on the porch than in my room because the walls hold the mystical property of amplifying sounds. When this wing of the hotel was once a hospital, babies of Haitian men, voodoo priests, were born here. Loa, voodoo gods, visited. I'm in Number Nine, the mystery man several rooms away, is in Number Five. I can tell by the way Larry King is breathing that the TV host is coming off a cold.

It was on the second day that I'd met Johnson. Travel books published decades ago say that most Haitians are mahogany-colored. They're not, but Johnson is. He was respectably dressed in dark blue polyester pants and a buttoned-down shirt.

"Listen, my friend," he said, looking me over as I climbed down the hotel steps and beckoning me to come close, "Mr. Graham Greene was a friend of mine. Like that," and crossed two bony fingers.

Johnson said he would take me around.

"Do you want the one- or two-part tour?" he asked.

"What's the difference?"

"In the one-part tour I'll take you to the poorest of the poor, Cité Soleil, City of Sun."

"What's the second part?"

"Where they dump the bodies." I said no to a visit to the body dumping ground, but I felt I had to see Cité Soleil. It's called the City of Sun because there is no escape from the punishing heat. Years ago the last trees were cut down for fuel. The main road into the City of Sun is a wide, dirt track the color of black water, with open sewers on either side. Stores that line the track are nothing but weathered planks nailed together, topped by tin roofs. Men, women and children stand idly about, or stroll aimlessly, smoothing the ash-colored road with their bare feet.

When I went there with Johnson I saw a man gasping for breath, dragging a cart full of sticks, not for fuel but for rebuilding shanties that fall down when the rains come. The shanties, built one upon the other, extend for what looks like miles along the foul-smelling shoreline.

As my guide steered me down a path toward the shore, a hooker in a pale blue dress shrieked like a mad woman and rushed toward me. Johnson stepped quickly between us and pushed her hard in the chest, but not before she pulled at my shirt, then chased me like a scrawny chicken.

"One Dollar! One Dollar!" the hooker screamed. Later she climbed to a tin roof so that she could lift her skirt and better display herself. "Five Dollars! Five Dollars! Together!" Johnson pushed me in the middle of the back, told me to hurry on by.

"She's crazy," he said, contemptuously. "Crazy from the sun."

Later a man slipped through the crowd and took me by the arm. His touch was light and gentle.

"Come to my place, sir, and meet my wife," the man said. I said no, claiming appointments. I felt a twinge in my side, thought of my own wife and child. His shirt and trousers were old and torn in places, but I noticed the buttons were in place, his fly and snaps neatly tailored. In my hand he pressed a folded card, written in English by a nurse who had once treated him, imploring mercy from medical professionals to help him if they can. When I gave it back to him, he coughed and coughed.

Johnson jerked his head, leading me away. He wanted five

dollars for a Guinness so I gave it to him and he ran off. Standing alone in Cité Soleil, I watched as naked children pushed sticks into mounds of dirt near open, standing pools of sewage. I saw a boy fall out of the back of a little public bus and in the fetal position hit the pavement with a thud. He scrambled to his feet, and ran off as if unhurt. A pig rooted through an open sewer. At the wharf, gangs of dark men waded in the surf with white industrial buckets, scooping up crustaceans. Through broken planks in the wharf I could see men walking barefoot beneath me, combing the wooden pillars below for signs of life.

Travels with Suna

by Shirley Streshinsky

THE FLIGHT WAS crowded, as every flight in India had been.
Suna took the first seat she could find up front, while I pushed
on to the rear of the Boeing 737. Normally, I don't pay much
attention to the model of an aircraft, but before boarding,
three of my fellow passengers had proudly pointed out the
superiority of this particular plane. I had to agree it was obviously more up-to-date than the old, bone-rattling Fokker prop
plane that had carried us from Bombay to Calcutta. I found
a window seat just behind the wing and settled in, a little sorry
that my view of India from the air would be impeded by the
wing and engine.

The flight attendants were dressed in matching saris—the
uniform of India Airlines. They came around, offering little
plates full of anise seeds which I supposed were meant to keep
ears from popping on takeoff. I struck up a conversation with
the Indian businessman sitting next to me. Suna had been
telling me about the custom of arranged marriages in her
native India, so I asked him if he had chosen his own wife.

"Oh my goodness, no," he answered, as if I had suggested
something altogether foolish. "It is ever so much better that
your mother and father find a wife, for I was at university and
hadn't the time to look for myself." He expounded at some
length about the quality of his marriage, about his children,
about his life as manager of a company that had been American, before it was nationalized. The house he lives in, he said
with some pride, had once belonged to the American man-

ager and it had a tennis court. He suggested I should send my children to visit his family in his big house with the tennis courts and gave me his card. I thanked him, as I thanked all the Indians who invited me and my family to come stay with them. Then he returned to his Reader's Digest Condensed Novels and I looked out the window, fascinated as always by the sere landscape stretching out below, riddled with villages. India is the land of my dreams, and my nightmares.

Instinctively, I pulled my seatbelt tighter as we began our descent. I've always wished I were one of those people who feel flying is a kind of freedom, who are comfortable whizzing along in aluminum tubes at 600 miles an hour, bumping into clouds. My sincere wish for all travelers is that they enjoy the sky. Unfortunately, I don't. Even in this early version of the wonderful Boeing 737, I was not feeling terribly secure. We were to land in some little outpost between Calcutta and Bhubaneswar, and it seemed to me we were coming in altogether too fast.

I watched as the ground came up to meet us. I could see the landing strip, see one of the ubiquitous cows that wander everywhere standing at its edge. I hoped someone was there to keep it off the field, since collisions between cows and aircraft are not unknown. (Once, when Suna's husband, Rusi, was flying for India Airlines, the plane he had just brought to a halt was slammed into by a scooter rickshaw—no one was hurt, but the rickshaw poked a large hole in the aircraft.)

I glanced around to see if anyone else was concerned by what seemed a much too rapid descent. No one was. I took a deep breath to calm myself, tried to ignore our speed and the increasing roar. I looked out the window in time to see the whole back of the engine slip away.

Dear God, we were going to crash. I wanted to scream, but

I couldn't breath. It didn't matter; there was no time. I felt myself go numb. In a moment my life would be over, done. I covered my eyes and waited for the explosion.

We touched down, bounced once or twice, then rolled to a stop. I took my hands from my eyes and looked out the window. The main part of the engine was still there, but the huge piece that had slid off was gone. I knew it must be lying out there on the runway. All the other passengers were busy pulling their packages from the crammed overhead bins. I couldn't believe they could be so oblivious. Nobody else had seen what had happened, only me. It was going to be up to me. I sat in my seat, trying to calm myself, thinking about what I had to do, knowing I had to do something.

I would tell the flight attendants.

"The engine," I said in a choked voice, "Part of the engine fell off—it must be back there on the runway." The beautiful young woman with a tika in the middle of her forehead pressed her palms together, fingers up, murmured a *namaste* and moved on. I tried the other attendant; she did the same thing. They understood English perfectly well—why were they ignoring me? I waved to Suna, who pushed against the crowd to come back to me. She was Indian and understood Indian ways; I knew everything depended on her.

"Something terrible has happened," I said, choking out what I had seen.

"Of course," Suna said with the equanimity that had drawn me to her in the first place, "We must go to the pilot and tell him what you saw." I felt better then.

The pilot came out of his cockpit, along with the co-pilot. Suna spoke to them, then the four of us walked down the ramp and onto the tarmac. A crowd of people had gathered behind the gate, waiting to get onto the aircraft. Well, I thought, they wouldn't mind waiting if they knew what I knew. I noticed a very small soldier with a very large gun. In the current political climate, soldiers with guns were everywhere. Behind him, a sign on a small building said "Aerodrome."

The two pilots, silent, led us around the plane to the engine I had seen fall off.

"You see," one of the men offered. I didn't see; I looked down the runway, which wasn't very long, but there was no evidence of the missing piece of engine.

"Not to worry," the co-pilot offered, but he didn't say why.

"Are you certain this engine is functioning?" I asked, thinking now about the next leg of the journey on this same plane.

"I am certain," he said, in God-like tones.

Suna agreed. As the wife of a pilot, she figured that if something awful had happened, the instruments would have recorded it—and, though she was kind enough not to say so, we were standing on firm ground, perfectly intact. Suna and I wandered back to the tiny terminal.

"It is curious," she told me, obviously puzzled, "the pilot said that English women often report seeing an engine fall off." She didn't know what to make of it and neither did I, but since our only other option was to stay behind in an aerodrome guarded by a little soldier with a big gun, we decided to trust fate and get back on the plane. This time we sat together, in the first row of seats.

Months later, back in the United States, I found out what had happened. On older versions of the Boeing 737, the back of the engine acts as a thrust reverser, sliding to the rear and opening in a clam shell design in a roar of noise during landings. It is part of the braking system, and that is what I saw. When I covered my eyes to wait for eternity, I failed to see the "clam shell" slide back up again and lock into place. No part of the engine had fallen off; I had simply joined a select group of English women who saw what I saw, interpreted it in the same way, and decided they must speak out for the greater good.

Our husbands and our children find this story delicious; they tell it whenever we are all together, as proof that Suna and I are just a little bit absurd, that we are innocents abroad when we venture out together into the big, wide world. We laugh with them, and over the years we have added a few more misadventures to our repertoire . . . a hurricane in Puerto Rico, and a prison in Bangkok among them. But I haven't forgotten that whatever misgivings Suna had on that flight to Bhubaneswar, she was willing to stand up and risk making a fool of herself with me. And that is one of the reasons why, every chance I get, I go traveling with Suna.

Lost and Found

by Tony Wheeler

TRAVELERS LOVE THINGS to go wrong. Why do travelers go to India, Brazil, or Spain? To see the sights and enjoy the food? No way, it's India for the exotic diseases and Brazil to get exotically mugged and Spain to have your car stolen. Ever meet a real traveler who has not had diarrhea? Come on, real travelers start with dysentery as a base line, the only question is if it's bacillary or ameobal.

So I'm sorry to report I've never had any real travel misadventures, not the sort that end up with spending six weeks in an Indian hospital or standing forlorn by an empty parking spot in Spain or Italy. But there was that time in San Francisco with the Hertz rent-a-car. At the airport I rented a dull-as-dishwater, gray Ford Tempo with red interior, drove it into the city, and left it in my hotel's parking garage around the corner. The next day I took the car across to Oakland where Lonely Planet's office is located and parked it outside. In the morning we drove over to the other side of Oakland to see our accountant and at lunch time we went out to a nearby restaurant.

Come evening we drove back across the Bay Bridge to meet some people at a restaurant in North Beach. My companion, Jim, suggested leaving his briefcase out of sight in the trunk so I opened it and he dropped the case inside. We had a nice dinner (Afghan food) and afterwards I took a couple of Canadian friends back to their hotel, drove on to our hotel, and parked the car in the garage. Jim took his briefcase out of the trunk and I asked if he was going to take his bag of books and posters out as well.

"They're yours, not mine," he replied.

We looked at them more closely and realized they didn't belong to either of us. How on earth had this happened, how had this bag of books gotten into the trunk of my car? Then I looked around the garage and there, parked against the wall, was *my* gray Ford Tempo. The keys had been in the ignition and I'd simply driven off in somebody else's completely un-memorable, dull-as-dishwater, gray-with-a-red-interior, Ford Tempo Hertz rent-a-car.

In all my travels have I ever had a car stolen? Well no, but I did steal one once, and I got away with it.

~

Losing your bags is another question. British Airways, Qan-tas, Pan Am, and American Airlines have all lost bags for me at one time or another, though fortunately never for long. What I can claim with real pride, however, is the time I man-aged to invert this common travel mishap — my bag got there, I got lost.

I was in Indonesia, flying from Denpasar in Bali to Dili in Timor via Kupang, also in Timor. The flight was delayed, I wandered off from the terminal to make a phone call from the building across the car park, and while I was away an announce-ment was made that instead of flying Denpasar-Kupang-Dili-Kupang-Denpasar the flight was now going to go Denpasar-Dili-Kupang-Denpasar—the first stop in Kupang was elimi-nated.

So I happily flew down to Dili, thinking I was en route to Kupang, got off the plane, and hung around in the terminal for half an hour, thinking I was in Kupang, got back on board the plane when the flight was called, and happily flew off to Kupang, thinking I was now on the last leg to Dili. Only when we got up in the air and started to fly west when we should have gone east did I realize something was amiss. This was obviously the funniest thing the crew had ever heard of, but the next day I flew back to Dili and my bag was still there, waiting patiently for me.

~

Then there was the time I lost my ten-year-old daughter on the Paris Metro, but as they say, that's another story.

Poles Apart

by Georgia Hesse

WHAM! SMACK! WHACK! Smash! Thud! Shudder, creak, crash! I am nearly seasick in this coffin-sized, wooden box hammering into ridges of ice atop frozen Barrow Strait. The coffin is sealed upon a *komatik* (Eskimo sledge), the komatik is pulled by a snorting Skidoo, and I am buried under a caribou hide, stiff with icicles.

Icicles have grown over the eye-slits of my goosedown mask, and its rubbery nose is bent to the side, making me suck hard for air. Blood throbs under my toenails, wanting to get out. All my bones ache from the endless pounding. Oh, no; now my sore shoulderbone is itching. An icy wind wails between the wooden slats and pierces through my parka like a jet of needles.

I was trekking to the North Pole, 1,600 miles north of the Arctic Circle, where Santa Claus lives. I had been told I would certainly be among the first dozen women to set foot on the North Pole. I and seven fellow adventurers had also been told by expedition leader, Mike Dunn, that I "had a screw loose."

While I was stretched in my coffin, we thumped across Barrow Strait from Resolute on Cornwallis Island to Beechey Island. It was to have been a mere five-hour slide. Instead, it became an eleven-hour ride aboard a battering ram. Storms had whipped the ice into upthrusts called pressure ridges on which the Skidoos skidded and coughed and our sledges faltered; nothing for me to do but rise (clumsily) from my coffin to help push.

Was I clumsy? Also lubberly and, face it, fat. I owed that (but also my life, I know now) to the outfitters of High Arctic International Explorer Services back in Resolute. I had felt stuffed as a sausage even before Resolute, squeezed into two sets of long underwear (one silk, one wool), ski pants, ski mitts, ski sweater, lined parka, socks in silk and socks in wool, feet encased in those Canadian Caribou boots with stiff liners. In Resolute, we were swaddled in U.S. military-inspired outer Arctic gear: thick powder-pants, parkas with fur-rimmed hoods, all-obscuring down masks, mittens larger than Yogi Berra's catcher's mitt. I could scarcely toddle; looked like Bibendum, the Michelin man.

As I slogged over the ridges, I remembered a conversation with my opthomologist: "And will my contact lenses freeze at the pole?" I asked.

"Not until your eyes do," he answered.

"Well, now," I thought in my best Pollyanna manner, "let's consider something pleasant." Like what? Like the Englishman of the Adolphus W. Greely expedition who hacked off his own feet to avoid gangrene? Like James Fitzjames of the fated Sir John Franklin party (off the happily-named ships Erebus and Terror) who wintered *right near here* in 1845–46, and watched his wretched comrades perish, only then to give up his own ghost?

At 3:05 A.M., we spotted pointy Italian tents on the windswept beach of Beachey. We staggered, we tottered, we stripped off the few top layers and plopped down, asleep in our bags on the snow. Unlike Franklin, we were rescued the next day by Twin Otters and flew back to Resolute in about forty minutes, where we careened into the Arctic Circle Club Bar.

Our Twin Otters skied down upon Lake Hazen, Ellesmere Island, about 1,200 miles north of the Arctic Circle, where a giant rubber Quonset hut served as dormitory. Pilot Harry Hanlan radioed ahead (crackles coming back told him the weather was fine and we should make our pole attempt immediately). We flew off, refueled at Tanquary Fjord, and headed up the seventieth meridian for the 560-mile push to the pole.

It was twilight when we crossed the last headland of the North American continent and roared out over the Arctic Ocean. We were to land where there is no land. The Arctic is a crinkled white desert, cut by pressure ridges, and studded with ice islands. At 2:11 A.M., in noon-bright light, we landed at 89.07 degrees latitude and stepped out of the Otter, smack (well, 90 degrees is smack) on top of the world. Burdened with cameras and my own bulk, I clambered out of the plane into the white-brightened light, stepping on my sunglasses in the process, and then sticking them sideways in front of my tired eyes.

What does one *do* at the pole? First, I tried to find a bathroom behind a pressure ridge. My fingers refused entirely to rezip my Arctic pants and as I looked up toward our little plane the pilot was standing on the wing, doubled over, laughing.

Our group also did something neither Peary nor Cook accomplished, that was not contemplated by Fridtjof Nansen or Roald Amundsen or even Prince Luigi Amedeo of Savoy, Duke of Abruzzi. Raising the candy-striped pole we had brought along, we popped open bottles of Mumm's Cordon Rouge and downed it.

I toppled over and sang "Sittin' on Top of the World." From my vantage point all directions were south.

At 7:18 A.M. we skied down again at Hazen and spotted the tracks of wolves that had lapped around our camp during the long night. Carried away with the courage of conquerors, we feasted on Arctic char caught through the lake ice, drank scotch chilled with pieces of glacier (scotch-and-snowda), and turned in. The temperature sank, the winds whipped up, and as I snuggled into my sleeping bag I wondered if anything would ever be exciting again.

A Caribbean Tale

by Abigail Wine

THE FIRST TIME I decided to go to Cuba, I had been traveling in Mexico with a friend who was a lover of the revolution. On trains and buses he read to me from the diaries of Che Guevara. We finally made it to Havana on a week's tourist package. Everything was as we had fantasized. The students, writers, and hotel workers we talked to all spoke glowingly of Fidel Castro. The food in the hotels was delicious and abundant; the beaches were clean and sparkling; the Cuban ice cream was refreshing in the summer heat. As soon as I returned home, I began to plan my next trip.

I made it back to Havana alone the summer of 1990, and there I met Alan Rodrigues who spent a week showing me around the city. He seemed very cautious and aware of the police who roamed the tourist area. We never met by the hotel, but under a darkened archway about a block away. He would hand me his identity card to keep in my purse. "If anyone asks," he said, "let them know we are old friends or lovers." I told him I thought it was legal for foreigners and Cubans to be together. "It is legal for you," he replied.

Alan invited me to travel with him to his hometown of Moron to visit with his family, and travel through the countryside in my rented car. Alan knew nearly everyone in the town, and was related to many of them: siblings, parents, grandparents, great-grandmother, aunts, and uncles. We attended a party for his brother, Arturo, who had just returned from Angola. His aunt and uncle slaughtered and roasted a hog to

155

celebrate our arrival. We made plans to visit Isla del Coco—
a secluded island resort for the weekend.

Excitement was building up for the night of Carnival as we
wandered the streets watching the dancing groups rehearse.
Night finally came, and we joined the parade in a horse-drawn
carriage. Alan had suggested that I buy a flash camera at a
tourist store so that I could capture *todo lo verde de Cuba.*

Around midnight, we ended up in an outdoor cabaret set
up just for Carnival with tables, a temporary stage, and a tent
bar surrounded by a barricade. Alan and I were drinking beer
and snapping pictures of each other as we waited for the band
to come out. I couldn't wait to dance in this dreamy setting.
Just then, two policemen came from behind me, grabbed Alan
and pushed him into the tent. A few minutes later he came
out in handcuffs. One of the policemen marched up to me
and demanded my camera.

"You were taking pictures of us," he growled. I gave up the
camera and watched Alan being marched through the barricade.

I ran to his house to tell his family. His mother and I went
back to the police station. A man in a brown uniform met us
and, with my camera in his hands, asked, "This is yours, isn't
it?"

I nodded.

"Where are you from?" he asked.

"The United States," I replied, "I was told by several tourism
officials that it was legal to travel with a camera."

"It is," he said. I was relieved. Then he said, "Come with
me, please." He motioned me into a sitting room off the recep-
tion area and called another policeman to guard the doorway.

"What happened to my friend?" I demanded.

"Nothing will happen to him," he said, then added, "You

have a car, don't you?" I gave him the keys and told him its location. He walked away.

I could see Alan's mother through the open door, though I wasn't allowed to speak to her. I sat alone in the room for about an hour until, through the window, I saw my car being driven into the police compound. The man in the brown uniform, apparently the commandant, escorted me into his bare office. I saw that they had not only retrieved my car but had gone to Alan's house and had demanded my backpack and all my belongings from his uncle.

"How do you know Rodrigues?" the commandant asked me.

"Alan is my fiancé; we met on a trip I made to Cuba last year." This was my only lie, agreed upon under the dark archway in Havana. "What have we done wrong? What are his charges? I was told we had the right to be together in Cuba."

"You do," he replied. I felt no relief this time. "Show me your passport, please, and your visa." I produced them. "And where are your plane ticket and hotel voucher?" They were in safe-keeping back in Havana. Was I required to carry these with me? I didn't remember. I couldn't keep a frightened expression off my face any longer. He must have noticed. He fixed me with a stern look. "Miss Wine," he said, "you are here illegally, and therefore you have no rights. Now please open your backpack!"

"That is not true!" I shouted as the blood rushed to my face. "I have gone to great lengths to learn the rules of travel and to acquire the necessary documents. My plane ticket and hotel voucher are back at the hotel in Havana. My passport and visa clearly show that I am here legally. You have no right to hold me and my friend, and I will press my government and your government to secure our release if I have to go to

Fidel Castro himself. I demand to call my Embassy!" Now his face changed. Of the two of us, only I knew that the U.S. did not have an embassy in Cuba. There was no pause.

"Miss Wine, please open your backpack," he said again, "and show me the contents." Alan had wanted to see all my things, too—a natural curiosity, I had thought, in a society with so few consumer goods available. I had a feeling that the same curiosity held the commandant, since I was clearly just a woman with a camera and not a drug smuggler. Out came the bras and panties into the glaring light of the office. The commandant and two guards glanced at each other. Out came the shoes and the radio, the T-shirts, the deodorant, the dental floss.

Another guard came in and handed me my camera, empty and broken, along with the strip of exposed film. They escorted me outside without explanation.

"What about my friend and my car?" I asked.

"We are just going to check on his identity. Come back in the morning and we'll release him."

Alan's mother held my hand back to the house. I expected his stooped great-grandmother to spit on me when I came in the door—getting her oldest great-grandson in such trouble, but she welcomed me with a hug and some coffee with condensed milk, and called me *querida*.

At daybreak, we began our vigil at the police station. Three hours went by and there was no stirring. Alan's uncle came to see if he could talk to the commandant. Another hour went by with no word. He took me to the Communist Party office— the local civilian authority. A functionary listened to our story and assured us that we had done nothing wrong. However, there wasn't anything he could do. I called the car rental office in Havana. They said, "This is what happens when you travel in Cuba." I tried to call the office of the U.S. Interests Section in Havana but the operator told me that all the lines to the capital were down. We went back to the police station and waited, again.

About 4:00 P.M., Alan emerged. He had a black eye and a huge bump on his head. We kissed and hugged. A policeman motioned us all into my rental car which was now missing a front fender. He drove Alan, his mother, and me to the immigration authorities in Ciego de Avila — the county seat. There, it was up to me to explain the situation.

The immigration official asked me a few questions, left the room, and returned in ten minutes with an apology for the unfortunate antics of the moron police.

"But they beat up my friend!"

"Yes, we're sorry."

"And what about the destruction of my camera and rental car?"

"Yes, we're sorry about that too, though the government is unable to compensate you." He dismissed me with a warning to keep all my documents with me at all times. He said, "We would appreciate it if you would not tell anyone of this incident." He didn't want tourists thinking the government and police were paranoid or untrustworthy. Cubans were the only ones who were supposed to know that.

When we left the immigration office, the policeman had disappeared.

Alan and I missed our trip to Isla del Coco so we drove back early to Havana. Six months after I left, Alan was arrested and sentenced to two and a half years in prison. He had tried to leave the country on a homemade raft. I remember he told me that it is forbidden to own a compass in Cuba.

Camera Karma

by Robert Holmes

Isn't it always the same? When everything seems under control, Murphy will inevitably apply his (or is it her?) law. Professional travelers are particularly vulnerable and when photography becomes an additional element, the formula for disaster is virtually guaranteed.

When I was a youth, my passions were photography and rock climbing. During a break from my first year at college, I decided to attempt a technically challenging climb in England's Peak District. There is a limestone spire in Dovedale called Ilam Rock that erupts from the ground like the tooth of some massive prehistoric monster. The entire route was severely overhanging to the extent that if you dropped a stone from the top, it would hit the ground some thirty feet out from the base. Of course, I wanted to photograph the climb and determined that late afternoon light would be the best.

Together with Paul, an old school friend, we set off in my father's car and in early afternoon sunshine made the two-mile walk up the valley, crossing the river, and meandering through woods, to the base of the rock. We started the climb. As the afternoon progressed, clouds started to obscure the sun and the beautiful light I had planned for evaporated. The climb was also much more difficult than either of us had anticipated and I now had to contend with the added burden of useless camera equipment.

By the time I reached the top it was already evening and the light was starting to fade. The route was strewn with equipment that climbers use for safety protection, and for two struggling students it represented several month's allowance. There was no way that we were going to abandon it. Paul started up. His progress was slow, and whether we liked it or not we were bound together by the rope.

When Paul reached me on the summit the light had almost disappeared. The only way down was the way we'd come up, using a technique known as rappelling. A rope is anchored at the top of the climb and you slide down it. In this case, the rope was hanging free—and the slide down was through thin air, not one toe hold anywhere. By the time we had the rappel rope secured the light had gone completely and it was very, very dark. It was a moonless night creating a deep, dense darkness with no relief, as though every glimmer of light had been sucked from the earth. The cloud cover even blocked out starlight.

Paul went down first, hesitatingly launching himself into the black void. Within a few seconds a cry came drifting up to me, "I'm stuck. My arm's caught in the rope." Somewhere Paul had read that if the circulation was cut off, gangrene would set in within half an hour. I never did find out if this is true but Paul was convinced, bouncing up and down on the rope, and by now his arm had gone dead. It was a helpless situation: I was on top of the rock with no way of getting down to help, Paul had only one functioning arm, and neither of us could see a thing. Paul had absolutely no idea how close he was to the ground. Thirty minutes passed slowly, and he made a wrong move. He freed his arm and fell. Fortunately, he was only five feet above the ground! I followed even more hesitantly, and within minutes I was standing beside Paul, although I still couldn't see him.

My father's car was still two miles down the valley. What

had been a pleasant country walk on the way in suddenly became a major expedition back. I almost always carry a flashlight with me—but not this night. Paul was a smoker and had a few matches with him, which helped us find our way to the main path but soon they were gone. For over two hours we groped our way along the river's edge, often on all fours, arriving at the car well after midnight. We arrived home in the early hours of the morning covered in mud, totally disheveled, to face the wrath of my father who had just been to inform the police of our disappearance—and the disappearance of his car—not necessarily in that order!

~

Many years later, on another continent, I was photographing a story on crossing the Sahara Desert. In central Algeria I had stumbled across a village wedding and befriended the families, who invited me to the festivities, the kind of unique event you always dream about but rarely encounter. The wedding was due to take place in the evening and it was going to be dark. Very dark. Black people under a moonless sky. I always carry a couple of small flash guns with me, so that afternoon I pulled them out to check them. Both had been accidentally switched on during the journey, draining the batteries of every volt of life. Of course, I always carry plenty of spares. I had bought them from a supermarket in England on the way over but this was in the days before alkaline batteries were stamped with an expiration date. I put the new batteries in. They were dead too, every one of them. I rushed off to the only general store in the oasis.

Algeria had recently started work on a battery factory and in anticipation of its completion, the Algerian government banned the importation of foreign batteries. Unfortunately, the new plant was far from complete and in the meantime there was not a battery of any size to be found anywhere in the whole of Algeria. It was not a happy photographer who went to the wedding that night.

As the evening progressed, the festivities became more boisterous and the men started to dance around, firing rifles at each other's feet. Here was the light I needed. I set my camera on a tripod, opened the shutter, and let the light of the exploding gunpowder illuminate the dancers. It worked surprisingly well, resulting in far more interesting photographs than had I used the flash. Often seemingly insuperable problems can be turned to advantage.

~

My first major assignment for *National Geographic* Magazine was in the Hunza Valley in Northern Pakistan in 1980. At the time, I didn't have a lot of experience and bent over backwards to make sure I produced acceptable results. I heard one day that a respected and revered shaman would be going into a trance to make predictions for one of the villages. What a photo opportunity! I arrived at the village early to scout the location and find the best vantage points. I loaded three cameras with film and waited for the action to begin. Having no idea what to expect, I started shooting as soon as the villagers arrived. The shaman entered the circle of villagers, walking around and around, self-inducing a state of trance. I was shooting like crazy. The trance seemed to be at its peak when a goat was led into the circle. I kept shooting. Without any warning, one of the villagers produced a sword and decapitated the goat. The shaman grabbed the head and ran around drinking the still-warm blood. I had simultaneously run out of film in all three cameras and failed to capture a single frame of the bizarre incident on film. By the time I changed the film it was all over.

"Could you do that just one more time please?" somehow, did not seem appropriate.

An African Christmas

by Paul Theroux

ON CHRISTMAS EVE, 1964, I was about to leave a run-down bar in Lusaka, Zambia, when I offered two bottles of Lion Lager to an African couple I had just met.

"Merry Christmas," I said. "And that one's for your wife."

"Happy Christmas. She is not my wife," the man said. "She is Nina, my sister. And she likes you."

Shortly afterwards we were in the back seat of an old car bumping along on a back road. When we arrived, the brother said, "Happy Christmas. My name is George. You give me money for the taxi."

They led me to their hut. And then I was lying on a damp mattress, thinking: *There are other people in this room.* The following morning I saw they were children, four of them, snoring in a heap like kittens in a basket. I felt ill, I was hung over, unshaven, and my tongue felt like a dead mouse. I had been wearing a tan suit that was now rumpled, and a shirt that had wilted. I dressed. Time to leave. George put his head into the room. "Happy Christmas. We have breakfast."

They took me down the village road to a ramshackle bar. It was about nine in the morning, a day that was already hot. The ragged barman opened three bottles of warm Lion Lager.

"I don't want beer," I said. "I'd like something to eat."

"Christmas!" George said fiercely and thumped a bottle against my chest until I grasped it. Nina was swigging hers, as though to show me how. The bartender asked for money. When I hesitated, George said, "Christmas!" and I paid.

I bought a pickled egg from a cloudy bottle that looked like a museum exhibit, and ate it. George was soon ready for another beer, and so was Nina. I bought them, I felt very ill.

"Where's the *chimbudzi*?"

"Come with me," George said.

"I don't need you," I said.

He scowled at me and poked my chest with his finger the way he had with the beer bottle.

"If I no come with you, you run away."

I said, "But I have to go back to Lusaka."

"No. You stay."

Sometimes in Africa, faced by Africans, I felt very pale, very skinny, very weak, and almost incoherent. This was one of those times. I was twenty-three years old. By late afternoon, I had begun to drink again and became less alarmed; then I was as drunk as everyone else and we went back to the hut, where I fell asleep on the mattress that lay on the dirt floor.

In the morning I told Nina I was leaving.

"No," Nina said. "It's Boxing Day."

It was the first time in my life I had ever heard that unusual pairing of words. George was waiting for us outside the hut.

"We go," he said. His wicked smile meant: *Do what I say.* He poked my lapel with his yellow fingernail. "Boxing Day!"

At the bar down the road I bought two pickled eggs and beer for the three of us, and I smiled, and we clinked bottles, and we toasted Happy Boxing Day. I thought: *Get out of here.*

Other Africans showed up. George ordered beer for them, and ordered me to pay. They drank. They ceased to notice me, except when they wanted more beer. It was about two in the afternoon on a very hot day and I felt a rising sense of panic. I began to leave.

"George," Nina called out.

I laughed. I said, "I don't need George."

"He will not come back," Nina said, and I realized how shrewd she was in her witch like way.

"Of course I will," I said. I took off my suit jacket and folded it on the bar. "Here's my jacket, here's some money. Buy me a beer, get some for yourselves, and hand over that jacket when I get back."

Before they could reply, I left the bar. Outside, I glanced back. No one had followed me. It was then that I ran, in a desperate flight, realizing that I had very little time. I made it to the edge of the village and beyond. Some children playing on the road looked up, startled. It was an uncommon, even remarkable, sight in Central Africa in 1964, a white man running in the bush.

The Yi-Ching: A Yarrow-ing Experience

by Katherine Neville

IT WAS THE best of trips; it was the worst of trips. It was a trip planned for ages with my life companion and best friend, Dr. Karl Pribram (one of the pioneers in the field of brain science and cognitive psychology).

In June of 1992, a series of Karl's lectures was planned at the Sorbonne in Paris, the Liechtenstein Palace in Vienna, and Charles University in Prague. I had much deferred research to do in Venice, Florence, and Lago Maggiore in Switzerland. In the eight or nine years we'd spent together, Karl's lectures and my book or research tours had criss-crossed haphazardly. We were used to hugging one another on concourses, as we hopped respective flights. Our relationship resembled that of two schizophrenic leapfrogs. We decided to spend a whole month traveling together—no matter what.

"Ambitious" is an understatement to describe what we irrationally planned to squeeze into that single month. Two travel agents and a secretary were so exhausted trying to arrange our plane, train, and automobile hookups, they needed a break themselves. Undaunted, we tossed in extra meetings with all our friends and colleagues.

Despite the fact that the schedule filled a three-ringed binder—which should have been a clue—Karl and I were sure this trip would be the closest thing we'd had to a real vacation. Hm.

Our introduction to reality occurred at Eranos, that Swiss former hotbed of Jungian activity—though now rather deserted and dilapidated—which at one time spawned works by everyone from Mircea Eliade to Joseph Campbell. The three decrepit but history-drenched houses, surrounded by romantic terraces and gardens, hang on a steep cliff dropping off to the Swiss end of Lago Maggiore.

I soon learned that the center's director, Rudolf Ritsema, and his associate, Stephen Karcher, had recently completed the first major Western translation and explication of the Yi-Ching since the famous 1950 Wilhelm-Jung edition. After a week of hard work together, Stephen, his fiancée, Luise Scharnick, and I decided that, in order to capture the subtle nuances involved, I really needed to have my own Yi-Ching read—an inordinately lengthy process, when done in the "classic" manner, which is, after all, what "ching" actually means. So we spent an entire morning, counting and reading and interpreting the dried stalks of the sacred yellow yarrow plant in order to learn the direction—or even the destiny—of my own work.

Meanwhile, Karl—not one of your major esoteric junkies—was a little piqued that we weren't in town, hiking through the scenic streets, and doing a little shopping on this, our last day in Switzerland. Ignoring our mystical mission, he spent the entire morning, across the way in the impressive Eranos library, plowing through the "hard data" of Experimental Researches—one of Jung's more feet-on-ground works, since it contains hardly any alchemy, or supra terrestrial channeling, or anything fun at all. He therefore wasn't present when the final divinatory results came through for me. The Ching—with little of its customary reticence or mystical, wishy-washy, yin-yang uncertainty—said it all quite clearly:

"You are on the precipice of greatness."—Wow. The precipice of greatness. The place that nearly every author aspires to be. I couldn't believe my luck.

Though the Ching seemed quite positive about the whole situation, there was a small hitch in the preconditions. During this presumably brief transition period between my future greatness and my current state of relative obscurity, I would have to meet certain requirements: I'd have to learn to overcome my normal obnoxious, pushy, lead-the-band, Mars-like aggressiveness. Instead, the Ching told me I would be required to submit myself with humility to the fates, to go with the flow, to become relaxed and receptive, like a damp piece of marshland—and further, if I did so, then quite soon the fabulous, creative energies would start to channel through me, impregnating me like a mare with her backside to the wind. In short, I would be able to "give good book."

Needless to say, despite these seemingly pointless conditions, the mere thought that I would soon do something really great made me feel I was walking on a cloud. At least, it seemed like a cloud at the time—and nothing whatsoever like a precipice. I left the terrace, rounded up Karl, and went off to have lunch at a charming restaurant on a sunny terrace, farther down the lake. But, as fate would have it, my divinatory prophecy was about to intrude—that very afternoon—in a way that would render the shopping question moot, render Karl mute, and nearly rend me limb from limb. It was only moments away.

Just after lunch, we went indoors from the bright, sunny terrace, to the dark rear quarters of the cafe, to find the restrooms. We were hunting up and down the murky corridors back there, until I thought I saw where they must be, at the end of the long central hall, and went leaping off down that pitch black corridor, into which—as Karl later remembered it—I simply vanished.

It wasn't a corridor at all.

The floor disappeared beneath me; I was swallowed by empty space. I thought I'd fallen into some kind of hole or pit—but I was still falling. I fell and fell, and never seemed to hit bottom. Immediately after that first sick, queasy feeling, when you know you've done something horribly—maybe fatally—wrong, I felt a second hot rush, one of panic, when I realized that my body was turning over, gravitating down-ward, so my head was below my legs. I was falling headfirst, plummeting down in darkness. I got my arm up, elbow crooked over my head, just in time.

When I struck, the full length of my body crashed against the steep flight of steps; the sharp edge of each step cut into a different part of me. Every bone, from my shoulder to my ankle, took a hit at the same instant. Then I was bouncing and skid-ding down, down, and trying to stop or brake the speed with one hand, while keeping my head and neck protected with the other. It seemed I would never hit bottom. While I was being battered by what felt like a thousand baseball bats, I recall that a quiet little part of me was telling the other parts that it didn't matter how many bones got broken, as long as I didn't smash in my skull. But even if I did, I thought with a kind of insane humor, I'm a girl who travels with her own brain surgeon.

It was lucky I'd been able to put my arm up. I was still mov-ing so fast by the time I finally skidded into the small hall at the bottom, the momentum carried me across the slick lino-leum, and with tremendous force, smashed me—elbow to wrist—into the far wall. Pain was shooting everywhere.

Then suddenly, the horrible idea struck that Karl might take one step forward, above me in the darkness, and plum-met down all those steps as I'd just done. The instant I could get my breath, I yelled up the stairs, telling him not to move at all, but to stay put and feel around for a light switch. When he turned it on, he saw me lying in a crumpled heap, thirty-five steps below. He seemed so far away. His face looked small and white, and absolutely sick from fear. I hoped things weren't as bad as his expression told me they probably were.

Now that I'd stopped, I felt more scared than when I was falling or bouncing. I'd hit the hard metal edges of those steps so many times, and with such huge impact, there was no way I could have escaped without at least fractures. And my sense of my own body made me suspect that many, many bones might be broken. I had fallen down enough ski mountains to know just how bad a fall can be—and this was worse than my worst imaginings.

My stockings, along with a good deal of skin, had been shredded from my legs. The gold earrings in my pocket had been squashed flat, ripping a hole in my hip. My ankle had a big gouge at the bone, and my shoes had been torn away. There was blood on my shoulder, leaving a stain on my shirt. I found I couldn't stand up by myself. When Karl picked his way downstairs and helped me into the powder room to look me over, we saw so many cuts and floor burns and scraped skin and bruises running the full length of my body, that I looked as if I'd been beaten by a street gang, and then roasted over a fire like a marshmallow.

So it was a precipice, all right—but what happened to the "greatness?"

That adventure marked only the first half of our thirty-day trip. After a quickie homeopathic-medicine healing by Stephen and Luise that night, the next morning, at 4:00 A.M., in drenching rain, limping with the help of Dr. Jung's former cane, I climbed the cliffs to the treacherous road above, and—after a half-hour taxi ride, a sixteen-hour Eurail trip with three train changes, pacing the length of those lengthy trains, so my injuries wouldn't get set in stone—at last we got off the train in Prague, the very afternoon of the day they'd voted to dissolve the country. (Since our host was Ivan Havel, Vaclav's brother, that was more than a drag—but that's another story.) After two weeks of marching in agony through all the narrow, cobbled streets of Prague, after climbing, each day, four flights of marble steps to our palace-like apartment ... one day, suddenly, it happened. It came to me, as if by magic.

For five years, I'd been racking my brain trying to figure out how to do it—how to write a sequel to my book, *The Eight*. I'd been reinforced in this mission by a bombardment of letters from bookstores and publishers and fans all over the world, who wanted to know what would happen next. And now I knew—not just in general terms, but in detail and living Technicolor. I knew what happened to each of the sixty-four characters, over the entire 250 years of the plot. So it was really a piece of cake.

All I had to do, it seemed, in order to meet those Yi-Ching conditions, was to step off the precipice—let myself be yanked down that rabbit-hole, as Alice did. I had to close one door on the known, the concrete, the world of the planned and self-controlled, and to open another, to a different kind of landscape. A holographic landscape of the mind.

Greatness, it seemed, called for enormous flexibility—the kind you needed, in order to fall into another dimension of thought, and survive. A graphic demonstration which I hoped I wouldn't need again soon.

When I got home, the first thing I did was to plant a sea of yarrow in my garden. Each summer, it comes up everywhere, as yellow as a Chinese river. Every time I look up from my work, it will be there, a gentle reminder to go with the flow.

And if that ain't great—what is?

The Existential Washing Machine

by Adrianne Marcus

Paris: humid in July, but still lovely. Excitement overrides the weather the first day. After all, our daughter, who lives here, has managed to find us an apartment to rent in Paris. We take in our new neighborhood: ethnically diverse, definitely lower middle class. I note the Alsatian restaurant downstairs, a Suma market just up the street, and most important of all, a Boulangerie on the corner. We will survive.

I am, as they say, *enchantée,* even though it begins raining hard. The umbrella is still in my suitcase. But never mind; rain in Paris is much more exotic than rain in the United States. It sings down from the heavens differently and, as we dash inside lugging our brick-laden suitcases up the two well-worn, spiraling wooden flights to the apartment, I am already making the adjustment from home, home to home, here.

Inside, more delight; here is everything we, as spoiled Americans, could possibly want: a television in a comfortable, if small, living room; a thin wedge of bathroom with a shower; and a tiny kitchen designed for elves, complete with a miniature washing machine!

The next day it seems to be getting hotter by the hour. But I am a determined American. We will see Paris. And we do. By evening, permanently glazed with sweat, we return home to rest, French windows open wide to let whatever air can circulate, circulate. The French newspaper shows a lead photograph of thousands of dying chickens with the headline: "Worst heat wave ever." I am glad I have come this far to see records broken. Tomorrow I must do the mundane: wash clothing.

As I study the washing machine, I am struck by a vagrant question: Must one be born in France to possibly comprehend a French washing machine? What could be so difficult?

I open the tiny front porthole, shove clothes in, add detergent, and close the door. Instead of words on the front buttons, there seem to be a lot of "universal symbols." Symbol for button four seems to be a mixed load. I double check. Yes. Symbol one is heavy wash. Symbol two is white. Symbol three is incomprehensible, but symbol four has to be a mixed wash or a *salad niçoise*. Symbol five seems to be polyester or cotton with a line through it. Wash and tear?

At 10:08 A.M. I turn the machine on. Half full of water, the drum begins to rotate. First one way, clockwise. Swish, swish, swish. Then a long pause. Then, counter clockwise. Swish, swish, swish. Stop. Visually intriguing, but after five minutes, monotonous. I leave to read the morning *Herald Tribune.*

At noon, I go into the kitchen to make lunch. The washing machine is now at level five. It is still going swish, swish, stop. Swish, swish, stop. First one way, then the other. This seems to be taking a long time.

The apartment is getting hotter. Paris is closing down because of the heat. By 2:00 P.M., the little washer has only moved to level six. I look at the dial again. It has thirteen buttons, or settings. One of these settings looks like the sun. I call my daughter and ask her if this is not taking too long. She assures me that French washing machines are very energy efficient and take more time to get a wash done than those in America. I can't see how five hours is energy efficient.

2:30 P.M. We leave to go to the Musée d'Orsay. I spend the rest of the afternoon reveling in Art Nouveau, Art Deco, and any art that doesn't have a swish, swish, swish, stop. We meet our daughter for dinner and laugh about the machine. It's still very hot out. I could certainly use those clean clothes, as could the rest of the city which eschews deodorant.

9:00 P.M. The machine is now on seven. Swish, swish, swish. Stop. My clothes must be shreds by now. Or all one color of shreds, I realize. I move the machine to eight. It refuses to give the clothes up. It does nothing but hum. I try opening the door. It does not open; some safety feature no doubt, to keep the entire apartment from flooding. How do I get my clothes back?

At 10:30 P.M. I am desperate. The machine keeps swishing, the water keeps going around, and we still can't get our clothes out. I am transfixed. I keep going in and checking it, like a new mother watching her infant. Only this *enfant terrible* is holding our clothes hostage. And we can't even communicate: ask what it wants to release them. I call my daughter, wake her up. She doesn't know. She doesn't have a washing machine in her apartment.

12 midnight. In a virtual panic, I move the machine to thirteen. Our clothes have been sloshing around since morning. I go to bed, desolate, imagining mildew, tatters of underwear. Tomorrow I will go out and buy new clothes. My favorite cotton sweater is probably a thing of the past. I let out a stifled sob. I now understand existentialism perfectly. Thank you, Jean Paul Sartre.

12:15 A.M. I wake up. There is no noise. No swish, swish. I rush into the kitchen. Attempt to open the door. Machine has stopped but it will not release the clothes. Dejected, I slump back towards the bedroom. Perhaps I can learn not to sweat.

12:30 A.M. I hear a click. I jump up. Oh joy! The machine has finally given up. The hostages are released.

The next morning my daughter casually remarks: "I guess

I forgot; French washing machines have this timed release. The door will only open fifteen minutes after the cycle is complete." Or after Americans have committed suicide. Whichever comes first.

Donner Party

by Scott Christopher Green

IN 1987 THE trek from Berkeley to Donner Lake in the Sierras, was my first of many annual retreats. Something about bonding. That's all I remember being told. Our collective anxiety fueled conversation for a few exits but thereafter the heat dictated silence. Route 80 was a parking lot, and with each acceleration and subsequent brake, our freshmen group would slide, then stick, to the vinyl seats of a blue '83 Honda Civic. Every sign for Route 80 seemed unfair, the number a bit too small for the challenge. Route 8,000. There, much better. To pack five, ripe, panting freshmen in the smallest car, give them a poorly scaled map, and have them leave directly from practice (no shower) during Friday rush hour, I now understand is tradition for the Berkeley men's gymnastics team. And as we sat on Route 8,000, in the distorted sweat-soaked city of Sacramento, I cursed my older teammates and their "see you up there" big brotherly wave.

The pilgrimage of colored metal lay like a wool blanket on 8,000. I resided in the space that has affectionately been referred to as the hump. Sadly enough, this spot in the car doesn't carry the same promise that its name does. Here on the hump, your legs are bent twice as far as the other back seat patrons. This forces the color from your kneecaps, leaving behind that unhealthy yellow that accompanies circulation disorders. Here on the hump, what little air that makes its way into the car travels a path that weaves somehow behind you (after it hits the other four passengers), neglecting to refresh you at all. Here on the hump, you are forced to bob and weave your head like a puppet, controlled solely by the driver who struggles to see out the back window through a rear view mirror full of your reflection. Here on the hump, like little knives, hair from the legs flanking you torments, tickles, and tangles with yours.

Evan, the thinker from Philadelphia, insisted that to make good time we should not only relieve ourselves before we left, but pack food to eat in the car. I brought grapes, an apple, and a granola bar. By the time I realized I wasn't just miserable, but hungry as well, the fruit had become soft, warm, and unsettlingly brown. I had at least expected my prize apple to resist as I clamped down on its weathered skin, but it gave way immediately. A warm mealy ferment of apple dribbled down my chin. No need to try the grapes. There must be an unwritten law of travel that states: "With five men in a car, in traffic, in ninety-five degree heat, a tuna fish sandwich is unlawful." Evan unfortunately did not subscribe to the same code of travel ethics as I, and proceeded to nurse a souring tuna heavy on the mayo, with wilted lettuce on wheat.

Black seemed a poor choice of color for pavement. Why not light blue? Or yellow? These colors would reflect the sun, and be easier to see at night. My thoughts jumped from hunger, to Sartre's *No Exit*, to claustrophobia, to "why me?" and finally to the lingering smell of tuna fish baking in the unruly August heat. We had been on the road now for about an hour and a half and had it not been for Cory's exclamatory infatuation with roadkill, I might have actually dozed off.

"That's four squirrels, and a raccoon," he shouted. My hope was melted by the scorch of the sun and his distraction with the deceased. "No," correcting himself almost immediately, "that was only three squirrels." He then explained, "You see the traffic is moving too slowly and you can be lulled into counting the same road kill twice."

Andrew sat in the passenger seat and had an AM radio to keep him company. To this day I understand that it wasn't Andrew's fault that we were baking like muffins in a tin. Nor his fault that the traffic seemed surreal. But, "I'm All Out of Love," 1979 Air Supply was unforgivable. The only thing remotely appealing was the name of the group due our circumstance. Evan suggested a game of geography, then twenty questions, but as soon as we began to play the volume was raised another level. My every breath was soon controlled by the rhythm of another love song from the seventies. The music, the heat, the tuna were all trapped, and somehow merging. Andrew insisted on "singing" despite booing and hissing from the back seat. He knew most of the words, mumbling whenever appropriate. Methodically we inched our way through the suburbs of Sacramento.

The startling sound of a horn cut through my misery. I turned to find a BMW carrying a balding man in a suit, instructing Chris to pull up so he could get behind us. I knew this man well ... he was the hunter: the man in every traffic jam who hunts the fastest lane. Again the shrill of his brass attacked. Make no mistake, a horn in traffic and heat of this magnitude is a weapon. Our antagonist would pay the only way we knew how. Chris put the car in neutral, pulled up on the emergency brake, and refused to move. The other lanes inched along and we watched the pain and frustration of the hunter as his lane faltered behind our Civic. The space in front of us grew, and with every car length his lips pursed and his fists clenched about his steering wheel. The beauty was that he had already established himself as a hunter, and was receiving no consideration for his blinker from his previous prey.

With a good half mile open in front of us, Chris began to accelerate. With confidence he smiled and waved at the hunter.

We abruptly came to a halt, thirty seconds later. My face began to radiate, beads of sweat appeared beneath my nose, and the smell of tuna loomed. The three of us in the back seat jockeyed for leg room, but knew there was none to be had. We had covered at least a mile in the last hour, which was better than the hour before. I informed Cory that he had missed a road kill, but I couldn't identify the species so it didn't count. I wasn't aware that there were actually rules to this "game" but he was adamant. So be it. I knew the heat had conquered me. I normally make a point to look away when I happen upon a dead animal. Now, I was inspecting the carrion carefully, desperately trying to make a positive identification. I closed my eyes tightly as the salted sweat rolled from my brow—the salinity was definitely stronger now— and opened them to sparkles of red and white on the horizon. All first hand accounts of death revolve around lights. I briefly wondered if my time had come.

Paramedics and firemen scrambled about tending to four cars tangled with a guardrail by the Vacaville exit. The traffic was being funneled onto the dirt shoulder, to avoid the gas spill covering all five lanes. Drivers seemed to soften in wake of the accident's severity. Gasoline rainbows glistened, eager to ignite below a setting, but still powerful, sun. I knew that every motorist in every car would blame the traffic on the rubberneckers, yet take ample time to look for themselves. The damage was devastating. One car stood upside down, and another was on its side facing the wrong way in the fast lane. Chris tried to watch the shoulder, yet his eyes jumped back and forth. Andrew reached over and pulled his seatbelt across his chest and inserted the buckle, dimming the seatbelt indicator light for the first time. Evan claimed he had seen a worse accident just a few months earlier, and I ... I questioned the existence of a God who would tolerate such horror, and then thanked him promptly for the relative smoothness of our trip.

We finally reached the foothills of the Sierras at 9:18, and fashioned our way through moonlit, evergreen hills. The road sliced through what I believed to be the most beautiful mountains I'd seen. I had spectator guilt, and I feared that the trees and mountains were somehow disappointed in my arrival. The mountains seemed wise, much wiser than the trees, yet welcomed the trees to stand atop for their lifetime. That type of giving humans will never be capable of.

Donner Lake 20. We have all grown to assume that the number following a destination on a street sign indicates distance in miles, but today I was more skeptical than ever. Our journey had been tedious, and I wondered if the measurement came in the form of hours or days.

We sped through the mountains, eager to see Donner Lake. I was the first to catch a glimpse of the water as we neared our exit. The heat had subsided, my legs had adjusted to the hump, and the smell of tuna, still present, was not nearly as troublesome.

Donner Lake 15. Evan informed us that in 1846, the first recorded act of cannibalism in the United States was committed near Donner Lake by a snowbound emigrant party. Donner Lake 12. Chris, I don't believe would have eaten me to save his own life, Cory, I'm not so sure about. Donner Lake 10. Andrew faded out a duet of static and Carly Simon. Silence and expectation turned my stomach. Donner Lake 8. "Five squirrels, two raccoons, and a deer ... almost double digits." Donner Lake 4. Life travel is cyclical. Destinations I'm afraid are linear. Tuna baggy on my foot. Donner Lake 2. Downshift ... Donner Lake 1.

Somewhere Under the Rainbow

by Barbara Kingsolver

THE ZENITH OF my twenty-city book tour for *Pigs in Heaven* was a night to remember. I was in New York for one day, and my publisher, Bill Shinker of HarperCollins, along with the head of publicity, Jane Beirn, and my agent, Frances Goldin, announced they were taking me out for a triumphant celebration. Our destination was a big secret. You can imagine how flattering it felt to be whisked away in a limousine following my reading to a packed house at Shakespeare and Company in Manhattan.

I should explain, before going on, that my dress code on the road is to pare down to the bare essentials. It's not practical to check luggage when you're on a multicity tour; you are on a plane every single day, and time is impossibly tight. When I'm on tour I carry one change of clothes with small variations. My uniform has to be very durable. For this tour I'd adopted nice black jeans, silk shirts, and hightop red suede sneakers. The sneakers, purchased in the Canary Islands, are about as elegant as it gets for a woman who doesn't do high heels. I'd also acquired a tie sporting silk-screened pigs. I'd been wearing this outfit so long I wasn't even conscious of it.

A book tour resembles boot camp. You often work fourteen-hour days, doing interviews and signings and readings in a different city each day. Because the whole journey can be a little like slavery, publishers go out of their way to make sure at least when you crash into bed at night, you crash like royalty. They put you up in five-star Ritz-Carlton's and Omnis so you won't be tempted to go AWOL. The treats make it all worthwhile.

So I was understandably excited as the limo headed uptown to our mysterious destination. We pulled up to Rockefeller Center. I was completely snowed by this fabulous art deco facade. In the elevator my ears popped on the twentieth floor and again on the fortieth floor as we glided to the top. We were headed to the Rainbow Room, the perfect place to celebrate my first *New York Times* bestseller.

As we walked across the terrazzo floor the maitre d' approached with a polite body-block, looked down the full length of his nose and said, "I assume you are aware of our dress code."

We looked at each other in bewilderment and confessed we didn't.

"No jeans. No sneakers."

He turned to Shinker, Beirn, and Goldin and asked, "Will there be three of you tonight?"

I was beginning to understand how right my mother was when she used to hint that a lady wears pumps at all times. As I considered slinking home in my substandard apparel, our ambassador of haute couture drifted off, leaving us to stammer and gulp.

In time, the maitre d' returned, and since I hadn't evaporated, he allowed regretfully, "It's a slow night tonight. I suppose I could seat you at a back table."

We followed him single file to a back table, which, as far as I'm concerned, was the best seat in the house, overlooking the million bright lights of midtown. My publisher sprang for Dom Perignon. I thought, silently, we'll show them to treat us crummy. We'll order expensive champagne.

But as I toasted the town in my jeans and sneakers I began to feel cheered. My mother also used to say: be yourself. Our mood caught on. One of our waiters rolled his eyes and explained, "This place was built in the '30s and they are trying to keep the mentality intact." Before we left another waiter whispered in my ear, "I think you look great."

Mom was right. If you can't be yourself, you're nobody. But even so, if I ever go back to the Rainbow Room, I'm wearing ruby slippers.

The "Daggy" Challenge

by Christopher P. Baker

"Best turn around now, mate. If you get through I'll buy ya a pint . . . and I'll throw in my missus for free!"

Now, I'm not generally a gambling man. And I don't normally risk my life for a beer and another man's wife. When a worldly Australian says a road can't be driven, I'm prepared to believe him. He described the route—a thirty-mile stretch of Pacific coast between Uvita and Punta Mala, mid-way down the western seaboard of Costa Rica—as a "daggy" (a dirty lump of wool at the back end of a sheep).

I took a more charitable view. I'd spent the last month perfecting my four-wheel driving techniques over, around, and across terrain that would have challenged a goat. Sure, it was still the wet season when, according to all the guidebooks, only horses and tractors could negotiate the track along the jungled shoreline. But as long as I could resist being carried off into the mangroves by the mosquitoes, I reckoned I could get through. My alternative was to follow the paved road inland via the Valle de El General then back to the coast, a 150-mile detour. That felt like cheating.

It wasn't long before my pulse began to quicken. The level road designed to shake the fillings from my teeth soon deteriorated into a narrow trail. Rain had been belting down for two days, and the mud was inches-deep as I slalomed north from the banana-town of Palmar Norte, where the Pan-American Highway turns east towards the Valle de El General. Not far up the road, I barreled past a Toyota Tercel full of anguished-looking young surfers coming the other way. Their car was out-skating Torvill and Dean.

Further along, on a steep hill slippery with thick gloppy mud, a truck lay heeled menacingly at an impossible angle, half on and half off the trail. A tree lay across the road, and the truck's occupants were attacking it mercilessly. *Thwack. Thwack. Thwack.* The sound of their hatchets on hardwood echoed through the great cathedral forest.

After bypassing that obstacle there were no more vehicles. No villages or farms. Not another soul for miles. The only sounds were the bellows of howler monkeys, the screechings of toucans and parrots, and the crashing of surf where the track briefly came down the coast. A claustrophobic tangle of rain forest had closed over my head. And for all the world I could have been the only person in it.

The trail was steeper than a dentist's bill with twice as many cavities. In places, razor-edged flint and sharp boulders had tumbled down the mountainside and had to be manhandled out of the way.

"Aaawright! I'm through!" I chimed, looking down into a canyon which seemed to descend into the stone ages, but which I sensed would disgorge me onto the surfaced road that began at the coast near Uvita.

Instead, the gorge descended into a morass of vacuum-like mud hemmed in by steep-sided embankments. The slough seemed fathoms-deep. Fuck! I selected low gear and inched forward. My stomach tightened sickeningly as the vehicle sank until it was encased so tightly that the doors wouldn't open. Yikes!

I climbed out of the window and sank up to my knees. When I extracted my left leg, my shoe was missing. I began dripping sweat like a faucet. Panic sweat. The perspiration of someone who had just junked a $40,000 rented vehicle.

Somewhere beyond the forest canopy the sun heliographed the heavens and sank from view. Blackness descended. And the rain forest was suddenly silent. Then the night noises began.

I curled up in the back of the Range Rover and listened to my stomach rumble. Why hadn't I stocked up on food? When dawn came, rain was drumming down from a sky as dark as Costa Rican coffee. I groaned miserably.

Fortunately, even atheists have their angels of mercy. Mine was a giant earth-mover which miraculously appeared around noon and plucked me free from my muddy grave. The giant "Cat" was one of several tearing up the rain forests for the long-awaited Costanera Sur Highway, a four-year project that will be a final link in coastal communications along Costa Rica's Pacific coast. I had followed the newly-cut path through the mountains and become stuck at its furthermost point. Beyond me lay impenetrable rain forest. My foolhardy attempt to drive through the pool had been futile.

I retraced my tracks and—tail between my legs—arced around the Fila Costanera mountain range to Dominical.

"Told ya ya'd niver git through, ya great dill," the Aussie said as we swigged beer together at a bar called Jungle Jim's.

"You remind me of something Paul Theroux once wrote," I replied, "about how when things were at their most desperate and uncomfortable, he always found himself in the company of Australians; a reminder that he'd touched bottom."

Beltless in Bali

by Burl Willes

THE LIGHT FROM the gas lantern in Nyoman's hand cast magical shadows along the garden path. Hand-carved, stone images came to life in the flickering, gentle light. Cicadas serenaded us as I passed through an intricately carved doorway and entered my candlelit cottage. How could a traveler's first night in Bali be more perfect?

In the morning I reached out from my bed for my pants, shirt, and glasses. All gone. Perhaps I left them in the bathroom in my state of total exhaustion following the long journey. Not there! And my bathing suit, shorts, underwear also missing. Gone: shoes, vitamins, camera, film, sunscreen, toothbrush, and toothpaste. There was not a trace of the well-hidden necessities: passport, airline tickets, and travelers' checks!

Friends called me to breakfast. I grabbed a sheet from the bed, wrapped it around my waist, folded the top down and under to create a makeshift sarong for my first day in Bali.

Beside himself with sympathy, Nyoman insisted that I use his shirt, sandals, and a more authentic-looking sarong. Buoyed by the good spirits of my friends, I was off for a good day of sightseeing, penniless and possessionless, 11,000 miles from home!

We reached the water gardens of Tirtiganga shortly after lunch where word of the missing possessions preceded us. With the genuine kindness and concern of so many Balinese my calamity created an unexpected opportunity to make new friends.

On my third morning in Bali the rice terraces were drained. Later that day Nyoman, beaming with pleasure, found me. Drying in a long row on his clothes line were my clothes, a California driver's license, a return airline ticket to San Francisco, a U.S. passport, and a festive array of travelers' checks.

After a dinner celebration, I lovingly placed each spotless possession into the empty drawers. Only one object remained unaccounted for. My night visitor, it appears, only wanted a western belt; he tossed everything else into the adjoining rice fields, to be returned by those who bring joy to traveling.

Getting Away from the Promised Land

by Evelyn Kieran

YOU COULD REALLY feel sorry for the Israelites who wandered around the Sinai desert for some forty years while Moses tried to get them to the land of milk and honey.

A more desolate place would be hard to imagine. Yet men have been fighting over this barren, bleak, grimy, hot, arid, ugly patch of ground for generations. Which only goes to show you that there is no accounting for taste.

We were a group of four writers: Robin and myself for newspapers, Tiffany, a sleek young staffer for a slick fashion magazine, and Rebecca, on assignment for one of the adventure magazines. A motley crew.

We had been traveling in Jordan—a dream. Jordan is a land of warm, hospitable people whose history began long before anyone thought to record it—except in stone. We had wandered through biblical places along the River Jordan, climbed endless gray stone mountains known to the first Crusaders, and stopped in small, stony villages where people dress and live much as they have for centuries. We had bathed in the Dead Sea, and spent long, lovely hours exploring Petra, the great "rose red city half as old as time."

We left Jordan reluctantly aboard the Farah I, an okay ferry boat that plies the Red Sea between the busy port of Aquaba in Jordan and Nuweiba in Egypt.

The boat pulled up alongside the dock in Egypt amid lots of shouts, commands, and arguing in Arabic, and the deck hands dumped all the baggage and cargo, including the requisite number of sheep, goats, and cackling chickens on the shore in the 110-degree heat.

We scrambled around, found our bags, gathered them in a single heap, and assigned one woman to guard them. The rest of us went in search of the promised "air conditioned bus complete with guide and driver" which was supposed to take us to a new luxury hotel at a nearby coastal resort.

The plan was to spend the night at Fayrouz and check out the facilities which the Egyptian government hoped would lure thousands of new tourists to the area. We would then proceed to the nearby Monastery of St. Catherine, founded by the Emperor Justinian in the sixth century and still in use.

From St. Catherine's we would drive in complete comfort through this little-known part of Egypt to Cairo. All the arrangements had been confirmed before we left home.

Or so we thought.

All the passengers and workers had left the area to escape the noon-day sun which was quickly turning the "port" into a veritable oven—and still no bus.

Also, no shade—anywhere.

Should we return to Jordan on the afternoon ferry? Should we try to find a public bus to Cairo, complete with goats and chickens? Or should we just melt into the desert sands?

A tough decision, when suddenly we heard the grinding of gears, the rumble of an engine and ... Wow! The Bus! Well, anyway, *a* bus.

We stumbled into the vehicle, trying to ignore the babbling driver who was busily tossing our bags through an open window while he apologized and explained we would soon be in a "five star resort."

Hey, wait a minute! That window was open? On an air-conditioned bus?

Something was wrong.

It didn't take long to discover what. Not only was the bus old, decrepit, and making funny noises that sounded like the imminent demise of the fan belt, but most of the windows were broken—to allow the hot desert wind to blow in all the dust, sand, and grime for which the area is renowned.

Then the guide started talking—on and on about the luxury of the resort we would visit, on and on about the places of great historic interest—on and on—and on. On and on struggled the bus. Deeper and deeper into no man's land as the overwhelming sun suddenly disappeared and it was night. And still we wandered.

Finally, the driver pulled over to a place at the side of the road where a dim, naked bulb spread scant light on the road.

"This is the place," he muttered. Out of the gloom a slim, self-effacing young woman appeared, flashlight in hand.

"Let me show you to your rooms," she murmured.

We followed her across the sand to where a few decrepit cabins leaned against each other, facing the shore.

"I'm sorry there isn't more light," she apologized. "We have no electricity from sunset to sunrise. Nor any plumbing," she added quietly. "Here. Let me show you."

"You have to do this," she explained, and reached for a plastic pail on the floor, plunged it into an old oil drum filled with smelly sea water, then spilled the contents of the pail into the toilet.

A covey of cockroaches screamed their way out of the light. We backed out in full retreat. The young woman handed each of us a key and disappeared.

Tiffany headed for door Number Seven, put the key in the lock, and tried to turn it. The key broke in two, leaving half in the lock.

Rebecca, meantime, decided she would seduce the driver into taking us to Cairo immediately, driving in the cool of the night. Adjusting her blouse and quietly palming two twenty dollar bills she set out to find the driver and the guide.

A few minutes later she returned, looking disgusted.

"They say we will leave at 4:00 A.M. They need some rest. Thanks for the money."

Robin and I just shrugged our shoulders and strolled up the beach. No one wanted to risk a run-in with the roaches we were certain held court in the dismal rooms.

Eventually, first light crept over the horizon and the guide and driver appeared. Sullenly, we piled into the bus and, feeling more and more like the lost children of Israel, once again we began wandering.

It was full daylight by the time we reached the turn off to St. Catherine's, and reluctantly the driver stopped the bus to let us join some other early morning pilgrims.

Standing at the crest of a long, steep hill, St. Catherine's is truly an historic treasure. Besides the Monastery, there is a fortified basilica, the Crusader's church, and the Chapel of the Burning Bush to commemorate the place where God appeared to Moses.

Half way up the hill, my aching back demanded a rest, so I paused with some other less agile women to catch a breath before continuing on to the monastery which was still out of sight.

Suddenly, Robin, Rebecca, and Tiffany appeared, going rapidly *down* the hill.

"It's closed today," Robin called to me, "wouldn't you know!"

Glumly, we returned to the bus. The driver babbled on about the virtues of the long drive to Cairo, through ancient villages, and past great historic sites. We couldn't have cared less.

Suddenly, Tiffany jumped up.

"There's a sign that says airport!" She screamed at the driver to stop, turn around, and take us to the airport.

"We'll charter a plane, bribe our way out of here—" she was nearly hysterical.

The driver argued, shouted—visions of the big tip he expected about to take wing. Tiffany persisted. We agreed. Finally, the driver gave in.

The airport was semi-crowded and somewhat modern, but there was no sign of a plane nor a control tower.

Tiffany and Rebecca charged in, demanding to see the person in charge. Someone finally indicated his office.

"Yes, there is a plane to Cairo, twice a week," he replied. "But I don't know if it is coming today or not. We have no radio contact." He smiled pleasantly enough. "Even if it is coming, it's probably full." He beamed. Tiffany demanded he issue tickets anyway.

"They must be paid in Egyptian pounds, no credit cards," he was firm. We pooled our dollars and took them to the exchange (for a suitable fee, of course), then he indicated the ticket window.

Over we went and, minutes later, this person appeared again, this time as chief sales representative for the airline. Solemnly, he issued the tickets. "I cannot guarantee seats," he warned.

Next debate: Should we wait the three hours until the plane might appear with possibly four seats or should we get back in the broken-down bus, and sweat our way to Cairo for the next six hours? Finally, we just flipped a coin.

Then we retreated to a corner, faced Mecca, and prayed a lot.

Allah was listening.

The manager spoke to the pilot who smiled a pleasant welcome, helped us on board with all our baggage, fastened his seat belt—and parted the skies.

Moses never worked a more welcome miracle.

Passage to India

by Helen Gurley Brown

A FEW YEARS ago my husband David and I were traveling to Agra to see the Taj Mahal, joining a group from the *Queen Elizabeth II* at Madras, India, later to return to the ship to steam on to Durban, South Africa. Arriving in Bombay with a four-hour layover before the flight to Madras, we checked into an airport hotel to shower, rest, and read about India and the Taj. In the room, David opened his carry-on travel case to discover an aerosol can of shaving soap had exploded, coating everything in the bag—address book, card case, calendar, shoes, ties, pajamas, hairbrush—you name it—with sticky white foam. For the next three hours we used all the soap and towels in the room, sent out for more, scrubbed, scraped, wiped, sponged, and swore, without any luck whatsoever in returning David's possessions to their original state. (The foam *liked* its new location . . . liked getting *up* in the world.) Without much time to spare, we had to tear ourselves away from scrubbing—so much for naps, showers, boning up on India—to get on the airport bus. There we had plenty of assistance—roughly five helpers for each of six bags (people *dress* on the QE2, plus I always scrupulously overpack). The assistants used up most of our American fives and ones—David doesn't carry change in *anybody's* currency, but no problem.

The problem is at Madras. We find the British Air attendant who lifted our tickets at Heathrow for the flight from London to Bombay has also lifted the portion from Bombay to Madras; no getting on the plane to Madras. You, experienced traveler, may feel the purchase of two short-hop airplane tickets not that big a challenge but we are not talking Los Angeles International or Charles de Gaulle airports, we are talking Bombay. Somehow the hoards of people—regular, old folks, teenagers, babies, many with goats, chickens, and dogs, all vying for the attention of three and a half Air India personnel, plus the bedlam, confusion, cacophony—none of it in English—and a cross-as-a-jackal husband sitting it out on a bench (like domestic chores, my husband thinks rectifying airplane mishaps is women's work) are getting to me, never mind how secure *you* would have felt in this situation.

So I stood in a hundred-mile-long line, finally got to the front where I wheedled, begged, and pleaded, to no avail, to use an American Express card and finally coughed up pounds. Returning triumphantly to my husband, he says the tickets are wrong—I've got us on coach. He doesn't travel coach from Memphis to Chicago, and isn't about to begin doing so in *this* locale—God knows the configuration of the plane. Getting back in line and "trading up" was actually a little easier than getting our tickets in the first place—by now I'm getting the hang of hanging out with goats and chickens. Once on board, the flight to Madras is uneventful except our hands are now breaking out in a rash. Using foamy shaving cream for brief moments on one's face is one thing, marathon scrubbing it off dozens of items is another. Onward. The Taj was super. Our first fifteen minutes there we ran into a dead man behind one of the mosques. Maybe they'd lifted *his* tickets from Madras to Calcutta and he simply couldn't take it.

First Date with Misadventure

by Richard Bangs

As a FOUNDER of Mountain Travel Sobek, the Adventure Travel Company, I've made a quarter-century career of ushering people out-there, to the front lines of misadventure, to the four corners and seven seas of worst travel experiences. But it was my *first* "well-planned trip gone wrong" that still pastes the walls of my remembrance.

My father never really cared much for the outdoors. He preferred a cozy chair and a fat book, maybe a ball game on TV, certainly restaurant food. But one weekend when I was a small boy he took me camping. I don't remember where he took me but it was by a river, a swift-flowing stream, clear and crisp. I have a faint memory now that my dad had a difficult time setting up the tent, but somehow worked it out and he was proud of the task. With some soda pop and our fishing poles, we went down to the river to have one of those seminal father-son bonding experiences.

The air told me first that we were someplace special. It whooshed, delivering the cool message of a fast river on a hot summer day. Then a muffled sound came from behind, back at camp, and we turned around and could see through the trees that the tent had collapsed. My dad said something under his breath and started up the hill, then turned back to me and said, "Don't go in the river!"

They were the wrong words.

At first I put my hand in the water to swish it around, and was fascinated by the vitality, the power that coursed through my arm, into my chest, and up into my brain. I looked in the middle of the stream, where tiny waves burst into a million gems, and then disappeared. It was magic, pure magic. I stepped into the river to my waist and felt the water wrap around and hug me and then tug at me like a dog pulling a blanket. Another step and the water reached my chest and pulled me down wholly into its vigorous embrace. I was being washed downstream.

Effortlessly, the current was carrying me away from confinement, toward new and unknown adventures. I looked down and watched as a color wheel of pebbles passed beneath me like a cascade of hard candy. After a few seconds I kicked my way to shore perhaps a hundred yards downstream. When I crawled back to land I had changed. My little trip down the river had been the most exhilarating experience of my life. I felt charged with energy, giddy, cleansed, and fresh, more alive than I could remember. I practically skipped back to the fishing poles and sat down with a whole new attitude, and secret.

When my father came back, he never noticed anything different. And I didn't volunteer anything. The August sun had dried my shorts and hair, and I was holding my pole as though it had grown as an extension of my arm since he had left. Only my smile was different—larger, knowing.

We didn't catch any fish that day, but I caught something that will stay with me for the rest of my life: a knowledge that the clearest way into the universe is off-the-path, upside-down, and downstream....

Libidinous Finns

by Linda Watanabe McFerrin

FINLAND IS WESTERN Europe's northernmost country. Further north than much of Siberia, it hangs, with Sweden, from the horn of the cold Arctic Circle, one of a pair of saddlebags straddling the gulf of Bosnia. All winter the days are locked in darkness. In summer, the nights are white. It was June. I was traveling in Scandinavia with Lawrence. Night after night I wrestled with the sun's flickering glare. Sleep-starved, I stumbled from smoldering midnights to shimmering noons, a somnambulist trapped in the endless river that flowed between these two cauldrons. Paris was our next destination. I longed for it.

Traveling by train, the trip to Paris from Orebro, Sweden would take twenty-eight hours. I sleep well on trains. The dark rattle of a railcar carriage has always been soothing to me. But we had a problem with bookings, and at the Orebro station, instead of the comfortable bunks of a first class compartment, we were faced with a cramped second class compartment. Six seats upholstered in dirty brocade crowded two of the facing walls. The green floor was marbled in grime. When we slid open the door, an explosion of sulfurous, sweat-heavy heat engulfed us.

"Lawrence," I hissed, "This is not a couchette-lit."

"I see that," Lawrence replied. "It's not so bad," he added swinging bags and briefcase onto one of the seats. "We'll shut the door. Perhaps we'll be the only ones in here."

July in Europe—not one chance in hell, I thought. The

heat was extreme; I sat near the window, reluctantly perched upon the rim of the first ring of our inferno, praying that it would not get hotter, and that there would be no other squatters in Hades.

The first man to enter was handsome, young, and quite tall, with long dark hair and eyes like a Siberian husky's. He sat next to me. The second, also tall and angular, had curly blonde hair and skin as pitted as a lunar sea. He took the seat next to Lawrence. They appeared to be companions, or at least countrymen, for they spoke to one another in Finnish. They quickly opened a deck of cards and began to play a strange game reminiscent of liar's dice. The corridor outside the compartment began to fill up. Faces peered in, assessed us, and moved on. The river of students eddied and swelled, parting finally to reveal two girls. One was a plump redhead, her cherub-shape squeezed into a pair of black jeans and a black T-shirt. The other was a frail blonde with a face like a Botticelli Venus, except that there was a carnal glint in her eyes when she spotted the dark-haired Finn and pushed open the door. They greeted each of the men in Finnish, settled into the seats nearest the door, and chatted, girlishly, among themselves. The card game continued. The girls got up often, leaving the room in slipstreams of their perfume and returning to catch the attention and, occasionally, a remark from one or another of the two Finnish men. They were invited to join the card game, and after a while they all left the compartment together.

"They're gone," I barely breathed.

"They're at the Duty Free Shop." Lawrence replied sagely.

"Lawrence," I warned, "I have to sleep."

"It will get easier," he replied. "It will get darker. We're moving toward the sunset."

The Finns returned with their Duty Free purchases. Now

sweating heavily, they replenished their body fluids with the dubious aid of a fifth of strong whisky, taking long camel-like pulls from the bottle's too-small neck, letting the fiery liquid roll down their throats, and chasing it down with great gulps of beer. The compartment reeked with the thick yeasty smell of this enterprise. Lawrence, to my horror, had turned-coat completely. Finding his niche in the excesses of Dante's third ring of hell, he had become one with our cohabitants. He, too, was engaged in their card game and guzzling.

The chubby redhead had fallen asleep, her legs agape in a small "y" that straddled her backpack. The young blonde girl feigned sleep through slitted eyes, one delicate hand seemingly resting in innocence on the thigh of the dark-haired Finn.

Lawrence, hardly the guide I would have wished for, looked up from his cards and winked as if to indicate that his complicity was all a pretense. I squirmed in my seat and looked out at the countryside that flashed past. The blonde girl had slipped further into her semblance of sleep, her hand fallen incidentally into the crevasse between the legs of the handsome Finn.

"Jailbait," Lawrence whispered, leaning toward me with a nod in the girl's direction.

I smiled tiredly, thinking of the drawn look of my sleep-deprived face. Behind Lawrence the sun was setting in a bright scarlet gash.

"She's tired," Lawrence said, addressing the dark Finn next to me.

They began conversing, strangely, in English, and I felt myself falling into an abyss under the spell of language. Darkness closed over me.

When I awoke it was to a world of shadows. Lawrence was awake, his face alight with jack-o-lantern laughter as he surveyed a diabolical scene. A full moon, or nearly, washed the compartment in ghostly light. Next to Lawrence, the blonde man, obliterated by whiskey and beer, was beginning his descent, a long, slow slide toward the faux-malachite of the floor, as the redhead unconsciously claimed the entire banquette for her own. Readjusting himself in his new position, he let his head rest lightly on the toe of Lawrence's shoe. I noticed that Lawrence was laughing soundlessly, tears rolling down his cheeks.

"Look," he managed to rasp, indicating the compartment's far corner.

I turned reluctantly from the Finn, so delicately balanced upon Lawrence's toe, to observe that the tender blonde Aphrodite had grasped the hand of the other sleeping man and was moving it slowly and rather thoughtfully over her small breasts. He twitched slightly, like a large dog, dreaming. Then murmuring something, he slowly rolled toward her, covering her body with his. His hands, in the darkness, looked like white foraging rodents. She slithered beneath him, finding the fork in his body, and lodged herself there, arching into him.

His response was predictable. They had formed an inseparable sandwich, fused into a coupling of delicate pressures and delectable glissades. Then we watched as she pulled the man's jeans down over his hips and loins, and the near-full moon glistening in the compartment's dim corner illuminated the rising and falling in an ancient and irresistible rhythm. It was shocking. It was exhilarating.

In a rush of soft groans, purrings, and pleasant animal sounds, the movement in the chamber's corner stopped, the participants parted, re-arranged themselves, and exited, trysting again in the corridor for a slow cigarette. Lawrence, cradling the head of the man at his feet, eased it onto the floor. A breeze rolled in through the windows, thinning the civet-thick scent of sex that now blanketed the compartment. I fell asleep again in the darkness.

Morning, sour and bright, awakened me as we rolled slowly towards Gare de L'Est, arriving at last in Paris.

Salt Lake City by Nightfall

by Susan Dunlap

DRIVING FROM San Francisco to New York takes four and a half days if you make it to Salt Lake City the first night. Then your second night is in North Platte, Nebraska, the third near the Mississippi, the fourth in Cleveland, and the fifth finds you tired but smug in the Big Apple. However, if you fool around and sleep in until 5:00 A.M. that first morning instead of 4:00 A.M., you reach Wendover, Utah well beyond the dinner hour, and the Great Salt Desert is too foreboding to attempt before bed.

The last time a friend and I headed East in my old Volkswagen we were determined to reach Salt Lake City. Thursday morning we were each up at 4:00 A.M. and were on Route 80 by a quarter to five. No breakfast; that we would save for our first rest stop. When we pulled into Roseville we gave ourselves a pat on the back for having waited until we came to a charming town. Charm, food, and making good time, that's what travel is all about.

Over the Sierra, through Tahoe, around Reno, and on to Winnemucca for the lunch break. One dollar allotted to the slot machine, and another pat on the back.

It may have been there, in Winnemucca, that we interrupted the hands on back for the question we should have considered before departure.

"Did you," Mary asked, "make a motel reservation for tonight?"

"No need," I answered. "I've made this trip four or five

times. There's no problem finding a motel in Salt Lake City, particularly on a Thursday night."

And so we headed back into the wide, tan landscape of Nevada. We reached the border and Wendover, Utah at the edge of the Great Salt Lake Desert by six. Hamburger, Coke, bathroom break, and a brief return to the motel question. We could call ahead from here for a motel listed in the AAA booklet. But we were more adventurous than that—and cheaper. Besides, it was only 6:30 P.M. as we pulled out of town. We'd be in Salt Lake City before 9:30 P.M.

Three hours later we arrived in Salt Lake City, paused for a moment of self-congratulation, then headed along the first main street, looking for a cheap and charming motel. There were three motels on the first block—all with No Vacancy signs. But it was 9:15 P.M.; we had plenty of time. On the next block we passed another full establishment, but were buoyed to note the one after that had no ill-omened sign.

We pulled into the parking lot before we realized that the management here signaled its glut of tourists by turning off all advertising lights. It did, however, have a clock. Ten thirty P.M., it said. We'd forgotten about the time change.

It was several blocks before we came to a motel office that looked somewhat welcoming. Here, we discovered that not only were they, too, full, but there was a huge Mormon gathering in town and every other *decent* motel was booked.

It was after midnight when we found it: Bob's Motel. Decent or not, we were too tired to care. We could sleep anywhere, we told each other. Bob himself sat at the desk, a muscular man in his mid-forties who looked like he'd just jumped down from the cab of his semi.

"You want the five dollar room, or the seven dollar?" he asked.

Having both worked for the welfare department we knew what five dollar rooms were like. We blew the extra two dollars and opted for the luxury unit. A good decision, we thought, as we made our way around two guys lounging at the edge of the cement walkway by the five dollar rooms, their feet dangling into the unpaved parking lot, their hands wrapped around beer cans.

The seven dollar room was on the second of three floors. The night was hot, and despite all evidence to the contrary, we both hoped for air-conditioning—even one of those ancient rattling window units. We weren't looking for gold fixtures, we silently told ourselves, just a place cool enough to sleep.

The room contained a lumpy double bed (but tired as we were we wouldn't be awake long enough to disturb each other). We put our suitcases on the floor (the only available spot). I was bending over to unzip mine when I noticed the cockroach. I had lived in Manhattan and was no novice to the world of cockroachery. The goal of the roach is to slither into a suitcase, nest among the silks, and arrive in Manhattan as a progenitor of a new nation of vermin. Up on the bed came the valises.

There was, of course, no air conditioner. The window overlooked the stairs but at least it would give us air. Mary had started to pull back the drapes when she realized that our predecessors had mistaken them for handkerchiefs. Carefully, she pulled them shut and went into the bathroom to wash her hands. When she returned we shifted the bags to one side and cautiously lifted the bedspreads. The sheets were a memoir of our predecessors' joys and accidents.

But there's always a silver lining. Since we had to sleep in our clothes, we wouldn't be opening the suitcases. We allowed ourselves ever so light a pat on the back, before laying ourselves out in pine box fashion atop the bedspread. The room didn't matter, we assured each other. Exhausted as we were, we'd only be awake a couple of minutes.

We were asleep soon. And awake soon thereafter.

A metallic creaking came from above us. Bed springs. We laughed, not worried. The room above had to be like ours. And in heat like this the greatest passion would have its limits. We gave them twenty minutes.

The rattling peaked and died in fifteen. It was still only 12:30. We could get six good hours of sleep. With the residue of smugness draped over us like a sheet, we sighed and relaxed. That was when the door upstairs banged shut, as did the door to the hall. They've argued, we hoped.

It was another twenty minutes before the door banged again and the springs started to creak. And another half hour after that....

The next morning we shuffled bleary-eyed to a restaurant, and drank two cups of coffee before we were awake enough to call North Platte, Nebraska, and reserve a room.

The Worst Bus Ride in All Mexico

by Janet Fullwood

JANUARY, 1976:

I don't know which was worse—the fish juice, the pig piss, or the vomit. All three substances streaked the window beside me on the decrepit bus lurching its way over the mountains from Puerto Escondido to Oaxaca.

The only thing visible on this moonless night was the weak light of the headlight beams shining alternately on sheer rock walls and into a black abyss.

We had taken the bus because it cost the peso equivalent of just $1.63, while the plane cost a budget-busting $8. Money was in short supply on this trip, but our time was open-ended. Besides, the plane ride in had been just too hairy. Two passengers in the sixteen-seat Twin Otter had thrown up from the combination of turbulence and fear.

So here we were in this overloaded tin can on wheels, bouncing along like something out of a Looney Tune on an all-night, thirteen-hour eternity of dirt roads and hairpin curves.

"I hate Keeeeesinger. I HAAAATE KEESINGER!"

Sally and I had split up to let a mother and child take the seat across the aisle from other family members. I sat next to a Zapotec Indian woman with a big-eyed infant tucked into her shawl. Sally got stuck in the row behind me, next to a greasy-haired man with foul breath and wandering hands. Every time she tried to doze, his fingers started walking. When she swatted him and told him to keep his *manos* to himself, he leaned over and hissed into her ear: "I hate Keeesinger. I

HAAATE KEEESINGER!"

Then he would lean forward, stick his angry face between the seats and hiss it to me: "I HATE KEEEE-SEEEEN-GER!" There was no escaping this unpleasant character or his disdain for the Secretary of State.

The bus had left Puerto Escondido with every seat filled and a few people standing, and at every village it picked up more passengers, almost all of them Zapotecs bound for the Saturday-morning market in Oaxaca. Braces of live piglets were strapped onto the roof, along with dripping bundles of iced-down fish, baskets, and boxes crammed with fruits, vegetables, pottery, and who knows what else. Chickens, bound foot and beak with strips of cloth, were stashed under seats like carry-on luggage.

The driver of this contraption, the man in whose hands our lives rested, was a study in macho concentration. He had the physique of the Pillsbury Doughboy and the demeanor of a Hell's Angel, and his arms and legs thumped furiously to operate pedals, gearshift, and steering wheel. Every now and again his assistant, a thin man in a stained shirt, would lean over to mop his mentor's sweaty brow.

On we went through the night, gears gnashing, motor grinding, hour after endless hour. The passengers who were standing—and there were more standing than sitting down— endured patiently, bracing themselves against luggage racks and seat backs, absorbing even the worst jounces and bounces with no visible change of expression. I closed my eyes, but couldn't sleep, the conditions were almost too stifling to bear.

Yet there was no opening the window, not even a crack. To do so was to invite a spray of noxious liquids in the face, compliments of the fish and pigs on the roof. Poor Sally got hit anyway when a bundle in the overhead rack started dripping an unidentified liquid onto her lap. Every few seconds came another plop. She finally had to sacrifice her sweater, using it as a sponge to catch the drips.

We were going too fast; everybody knew it. The bus was careening on the curves, and you could feel the motor race as the driver floored it on the straightaways. An undercurrent of anxiety spread through the bus. I felt my mouth go dry and my fingers tighten on the edge of my seat, and looked over to see people in the aisles gripping the overhead rack and hiding their faces in the crooks of their arms. The man in front of me turned around and, with a weak smile, offered me a bottle of mezcal—vaccination against terror. I took a deep swig and shuddered.

Not long after, the hairpin curves began to take their toll. First one standing passenger, and then another was overcome by motion sickness.

I heard the urping sounds first, then smelled the smell, then felt a man's body leaning over me, clawing at the window. He got it open, leaned his head out and puked. Not all of it went outside; I felt a warm liquid splashing on my sandaled foot, but there was nothing I could do.

The stench and the retching were contagious. A nightmarish reek of vomit, sweat, bad breath, and tequila lay like a weight in the air. Even the most stoic of passengers couldn't take it any longer. Finally, the driver pulled over and everyone piled out—women on one side, men on the other—to clean themselves up as best they could. The fresh air was balm for the senses.

There was no choice but to force ourselves back into that moving torture chamber for the remainder of the trip. Hours passed, and the sky began to change from black to pale silver. At last the bus pulled into the station in Oaxaca, and a stream of weary passengers staggered out into a new day.

The Best Restaurant in Town?

by Marcia Muller and Bill Pronzini

Warning: Don't believe everything you read in travel guides. Some recommendations may be hazardous to your health.

THE GUIDE WE consulted a few years ago, when we spent a night in a medium-sized Idaho city while on a driving trip, should have carried the above disclaimer. Unfortunately for us, we believed the three-star rating given to a restaurant not far from our motel. No other received more than two stars; therefore, we reasoned, this one must be the best restaurant in town.

Its physical appearance and clientele gave us no hint of its true nature. The place was attractive enough, if undistinguished, and full of normal-looking people eating what appeared from a distance to be normal-looking food. A friendly waitress showed us to a booth in an alcove near the salad bar, the last available seating. And the menus she handed us seemed to advertise an array of traditional but palatable items.

We considered. One of us decided on the lamb chops, the other opted for Southern Fried Chicken; house burgundy with the former, house white with the latter. Did we want the salad bar? the waitress asked. A leisure-suited man at a nearby table had been loudly praising the bar's selections to his companion, so we said yes.

The selections did look fairly interesting—until another man, who'd gone up ahead of us, chose to sneeze without covering his mouth and sprayed the iceberg lettuce. This wasn't the fault of the restaurant, of course, but where was the ubiquitous plastic sneeze guard we'd seen everywhere else on our trip? One of us decided to forego the salad bar after all. The other, being a braver and more adventurous soul, gathered random samples that excluded the iceberg lettuce and anything in close proximity to it.

These samples were not eaten, however. The adventurous soul's appetite for salad vanished when the leisure-suited fellow missed his mouth with a heaping forkful of cottage cheese and pasta salad—literally opened his mouth to insert said forkful, only to mysteriously upend the fork an inch and a half short. The sight of the whitish mass avalanching down his shirtfront brought on a fierce yearning for wine.

The wine arrived. The house burgundy looked and tasted pink. Not a blush type, but that suspicious, sickly variety of "rosé" that as young adults we would buy for a dollar a half-gallon. The house white, which the waitress had assured us was very dry, was in fact very sweet and contained an odd, kerosene-like piquancy. We would soon drink them both anyway.

A basket of rolls and biscuits arrived. One of us selected a roll, only to discover that it was not a roll. It resembled bread, but it was not, nor had it ever been, bread. It had been made of a concrete-like substance that could not be broken by knife, hand, teeth, or possibly even sledgehammer.

The entrees arrived. The chicken was not Southern Fried. On the outside it was Northern Cremated; on the inside it was Prime Rib Bloody. The batter in which it had been rolled was flavored with a strange melange of spices and something black that was not pepper. The lamb chops—ah, the lamb chops! They were thin, gray, and rested on a large lettuce leaf. Something dribbled from them that may or may not have been gravy or natural juices; it resembled, and had the consistency of, crankcase oil. As we watched in awe, this liquid not only caused the lettuce leaf to shrivel but seemed to dissolve parts of it around the edges.

Our horror by this time had given way to a kind of maniacal mirth. Whispered comments on what lay before us produced giggles and snorts that brought wary looks from some of the other diners. We might have managed to maintain at least some public decorum if the chef had not chosen that moment to emerge from the kitchen to survey his domain. He was short and unshaven and wore a tall white hat that had been crushed on top and bent at the middle; his apron and his once-white shirt were smeared with sinister-looking stains; the cigarette that hung from a corner of his mouth trailed ashes; and the smile he wore was both self-satisfied and, so it seemed to us, quite mad.

One look at this culinary specimen and we lost it completely. One of us banged a roll against the wall, and not a flake broke off; this served to prolong our laughing fit. A nearby couple, who may or may not have been finished eating, got up and hastily departed.

We finally managed to regain a semblance of control. The waitress, who now looked as though she wished she'd taken a job at McDonald's instead, appeared to clear our table. With brilliant understatement and no discernible irony, she said she'd noticed we hadn't seemed to enjoy our dinners. For being such good sports, perhaps we'd like to have dessert on the house. She didn't elaborate as to what she meant by "such good sports." Possibly a good sport in this establishment was anyone who neither complained to the management nor attempted to bludgeon the chef to death with one of his nonbread rolls.

How could we refuse? We accepted with as much grace as we could summon. Our dessert choices, she said, were apple cobbler or bread pudding. Which would she recommend? we asked.

"Well," she said ominously, "I wouldn't recommend the pudding."

We both ordered apple cobbler.

When two dishes of it arrived we studied the brownish contents for a time. After which the following conversation took place:

"Isn't apple cobbler supposed to have crust?"

"Yes, it is."

"I don't see any crust in my dish or yours."

"Neither do I. . . . Wait a minute, what's that?"

"Where?"

"There. That tiny white thing there. Is that crust?"

"I'm not going to eat it to find out. It looks like something dead floating in a bog."

The description was apt, even if the timing wasn't. We were trying not to make cackling spectacles of ourselves again when the waitress hurriedly brought our check.

We left her a generous tip; after all, none of this had been her fault and she, too, had been a good sport. As we were leaving we passed a table occupied by half a dozen police officers in uniform. None of them looked happy; in fact, a couple appeared sullen. Outside, we vowed to scrupulously obey all traffic laws on the drive back to the motel and out of town in the morning.

If the local cops were regular patrons of "the best restaurant in town," this was no place to run afoul of the law!

Puerto Plata: Just Say No

by Barbara Ann Curcio

I JUST HAD the worst vacation of my life in the Dominican Republic. How bad was it? If it had been a trip to the dentist, it would have been a root canal.

Imagine a thorough education in the four R's of tropical travel: rats, roaches, rain, and rip-off. Think of a week so awful the highlight was the 9:00 P.M. nightly sighting of a mystery bus bound for "Minneapolis/St. Paul," (because you wished you were on it, even though it was the middle of winter). Think of the kind of trip only your mother-in-law could book you on (and did).

It was my own fault. I've traveled enough to know that you can't always trust travel agents and guidebooks. After all, Columbus, the very first Caribbean tourist, had benefit of neither. And though I read about his voyage, I hadn't read between the lines. Columbus visited Puerto Plata, all right, but he was smart enough to stay on his ship.

My guidebook described a hotel that was less than a palace, with "rather flimsy" construction. What did this matter? I would be spending all my time outdoors. What I got was Eurotel, done in "Pirates of the Caribbean" decor, less than two years old and already surpassing all notions of "planned obsolescence"—as solid as a Potemkin Village.

I could expect "invariably sunny" weather on the North Coast of the Dominican Republic this time of year, the guidebooks had said. What I got was weather with a severe case of PHS (pre-hurricane syndrome), and a week of torrential rains.

Our trip began badly on a "Gulf Air" charter flight, a name that spoke to me: it said "Hezbolah! Hostages! Hijack! (Run away!)." As we boarded, a crew member announced both the wrong flight number and destination. Gulf Air must have said "Mexico" to him, because that's where he thought Puerto Plata was. It was just that kind of flight—the kind where the woman in front of us in line for the lavatory went in holding a baby, and came out alone.

Our initiation into the Dominican Republic (one does not merely arrive) consisted of trial-by-immigration forms. The forms were insidious, the sort where you can't tell until you're nearly done whether your input goes above or below the line. Once reduced to the same level of incompetence, we were ready for our vacation.

We checked into Eurotel, our hotel, (*Who* did you say was on first?), to find that the accommodations we had reserved and prepaid for were unavailable. The hotel was overbooked by fifty rooms and we would be downgraded, explained the clerk nonchalantly, proffering a well-rehearsed sop: Why, we were lucky to have rooms at all. No, they would not give us a refund, but we would get free breakfast for a week, to compensate for the inconvenience. And there was a lot to compensate for. Take the view overlooking the garbage dump, an open cesspool and the nearby kitchen. Or the pervasive odor of yesterday's and today's dinner, relieved only by rampant mildew. Our daytime soundtrack, broadcast from poolside, was rock music amplified at wake-the-dead decibel levels, and the social director's frequent war whoop, "Arriba!"—which mobilized no one. Our night music was a symphony of smashing glass from the trash compactor, sounds of arguing at 4:00 A.M. coming from the staff quarters next door, and again at 6:00 A.M. as the employee bus, "El Mucho Macho," unloaded.

What it lacked in quiet, the room compensated for in plumbing, equipped as it was with two showers, if you count the impromptu one in the closet whenever it rained. During the frequent storms, the bathroom with its leaky ceiling, toilet, and tub, became a wading pool, and the walls oozed a white glutinous slime.

On an empty stomach and wearing earplugs, we could just tolerate our accommodations—until after 11:30 P.M. when the roaches began their nocturnal meanderings. One couple we met was so overrun they left all the lights on every night, and slept with blindfolds. And there was no use sleeping on the beach, with its plagues of sand fleas and millipedes. Even the local tourist paper was running ads for pest control: we wondered whether we could order room service.

After two days of Euro-torture and tag-team kvetching, we were finally moved to the promised rooms. This time our bathroom was under construction, the floor torn up and a gaping hole in the wall. But the previous tenants had spent two weeks there and didn't seem to mind not having a bathroom floor, explained the clerk. (Must have been Spiderman and his wife.)

Outside our rooms, a similar state of chaos prevailed. As the rains persisted, there was water everywhere. Leaks sprang from roofs and ceilings faster than buckets could catch them; the swimming pool overflowed.

In gale-force winds, tables and chairs left unsecured blew around like autumn leaves. Glassware flew off tables, and a glass activities placard in the lobby smashed to the stone floor, narrowly missing several guests. The personnel seemed unconcerned, save one soul assigned to hold onto the Christmas tree in the lobby, to prevent it from blowing away. Broken glass abounded, and only the most myopic janitors were on duty.

And did I mention the power failures? Or the garbage-strewn beach, and the rats grazing on the grounds under the banana trees late at night?

Exasperated, we tried touring. Due to the weather, our excursions were restricted to the nearby towns of Sosua and Puerto Plata. We abandoned plans to explore wilderness areas farther away, including a primeval mangrove swamp. In the ramshackle towns we joined pale-faced (not enough sun) tourists wandering glassy-eyed (too many piña coladas) from one dreck purveyor to the next. Shops sold indigenous art, T-shirts and maracas with the inscription "No Problem" and more exotic fare such as Toronto Blue Jays' pennants. As for restaurants, we passed up "The Best Little Boar House in Town," for "Oceanicus," chosen from our guidebooks, only to find it had been closed down by the Board of Health. We eschewed the more primitive sections of town, where, according to our guide, the inhabitants lived "on the river, with no running water, and by candlelight." It sounded too much like our hotel.

We hastily returned to Eurotel where, despite the tragic demise of the activities board, events were in full swing back at the pool: inner-tube, three-legged, and frog races; egg-throwing, watermelon eating, and "Mr. Legs" contests. And these were the adult activities. Not that we were expecting group discussions of Schopenhauer. All we wanted was the tennis, cycling, riding, and "water activities" Eurotel purported to have. But these weren't at our hotel (you had to walk to the hotels down the beach).

Attempts to socialize failed, as the other guests were clearly not our type. It wasn't so much the gold chains, or their delight in the potato-rolling contests. Their chief offense was that they actually seemed to be having a good time.

We turned to food for comfort, and quickly turned away. Service was excruciatingly slow, the waiters capable of amazing feats of customer avoidance. Their specialty was cruising the dining room, pirouetting in place without getting dizzy or ever once catching a patron's eye. (They must have spent months on this at waiters' school.)

We resorted to drink and took refuge in fantasies. We imagined being airlifted out of Eurotel and transported to Casa de Campo, where, at this moment, they were undoubtedly watching polo matches, or shaving in bathrooms with floors and running water. And we made up titles for the guidebook we would write when we got home: *Puerto Plata: Just Say No.*

All Dressed Up and Nowhere to Go

by Stan Sesser

MOST TREKKERS COME back from Nepal with glowing accounts of snow-capped mountains, cascading rivers, and warm and hospitable people.

I returned obsessed with shit.

While shit is the big unmentionable in international travel, that doesn't mean it hasn't soiled the memory of many a vacation. Bangkok, for instance, is literally floating on shit, with a high water table and raw effluent that goes untreated directly into the city's canals and river. The traveler who gets only an occasional whiff walking down the street is lucky; I've smelled the unmistakable odor waft out of the bathroom ventilation systems at the hotels. The glorious but decrepit colonial-era Strand Hotel in Rangoon did me one better: After flushing the toilet, the contents would come through the bathtub drain.

My journeys in Asia have yielded many less-than-pleasant moments dealing with eliminatory functions. In Chinese cities, most dwellings have no bathrooms and the locals use neighborhood communal facilities. They are never cleaned, and the stench, even from blocks away, is horrible. In rural Vietnam, farmers do their duty in lean-to's jutting out over fishponds, which kills the appetite for the fish commonly served at dinner. And in many Asian countries people use their left hand as a substitute for toilet paper, and eat with their right.

But no one else can make shit such an all-pervasive, inescapable experience as do the Nepalese. You'll never read it in a guidebook, to be sure, but the mountain kingdom of Nepal from one end to the other is paved with human feces.

I'll start my account of this less-savory aspect of Nepal by describing my climb to Mamche Bazaar. For the first half of the trip, the walk is repeatedly up and down, going between 9,000 and 12,000 feet. While the scenery is beautiful, it consists largely of hills and valleys, and not the soaring mountains we had expected to see. Consequently, we made no progress at all in acclimating to high altitudes, because as we got to a higher elevation, we would then have to descend.

This frustration ended with the road to the village of Mamche Bazaar. After a steady climb we finally arrived in the Everest high country, surrounded by the famous peaks.

The great highlight of this road is a little branch part, marked by a sign that reads "first view of Mount Everest." After about a quarter of a mile with no view at all, the path suddenly breaks out into breathtaking mountain scenery, with Mount Everest looming right in front of the awestruck trekker.

For the Nepalese, however, this viewpoint serves as little more than a convenient latrine. Why defecate just anywhere, after all, when you can shit while being diverted by some of the world's most spectacular scenery? The result is that the viewpoint is carpeted by heaps of steaming turds, many of them topped with pink Chinese toilet paper like frosting on a wedding cake. If you dare to look up at the mountains while walking instead of down at your feet, you're in trouble.

The Nepalese relieve themselves anywhere and everywhere, often on the road in front of their houses or, for the more modest, behind bushes. A particularly favorite place seems to be in the creeks that serve as the local water supply. The water coming from Mount Everest starts out as pure melted snow just a relatively few miles away. But to drink it, the water has to be boiled for half an hour.

Where does a fastidious American shit? Every day after lunch, I would slink off and look for a big bush that would preserve my modesty. In more populated areas, every single bush would be occupied, and I would engage in a race against time to find an empty spot. On other days, little children gathered around to watch. As I pulled down my pants, they stood around laughing and pointing. When that got boring they started throwing stones.

Then there is the bane of trekking in Nepal, another unmentionable: diarrhea. Given the level of sanitation, diarrhea comes frequently, and it means going through the embarrassment of finding a place to shit not once a day but once every fifteen minutes.

One of the low points of my life came not far into the trek. The rain was torrential, so bad that the guides couldn't consider setting up camp. We had to rent space in a "teahouse." Unfortunately, these teahouses are not nearly as quaint as the name implies. A fire burns constantly in the area of the house used as a kitchen, but Nepalese homes do not have chimneys and the smoke remains inside. Every surface of the house becomes black with soot, including the wood slabs that serve as the beds. To keep the occupants from choking to death, all the windows must be opened, so a freezing-cold wind circulates with the thick, acrid smoke.

In the middle of the night, I had an attack of the runs of unprecedented severity. Each time I drifted into a half sleep on the hard, filthy slab, I was jolted awake and had to run outside into the downpour. I survived that night by fantasizing about being in a warm bed at home, with a clean bathroom just a few steps away.

Of course, the trek wasn't entirely about shit. That was the downside, but there were highlights too. Our Sherpa "guide," for example, had never before set foot in Nepal; he was from Darjeeling, and kept leading us down wrong paths. The doctor in our group could do nothing because the trekking company had neglected to supply a medical kit. For the first ten days, the freezing rain rarely stopped. Most meals consisted of boiled cabbage with ketchup, washed down by Ovaltine. At 18,000 feet, I was colder than I had ever been in my life, shivering away while wrapped in a wool shirt, down jacket, and two down sleeping bags.

Oh, yes, and Mount Everest was magnificent.

So that's my story about shit in Nepal, a part of my notes that I never thought would see the light of day. Someday this might inspire me with enough courage to venture beyond shit into the subject of hawking. Hawking is a word rarely heard in America, but it's very common in Asia; buses in Hong Kong, for instance, have "no hawking" signs, not that they do any good. In Nepal, hawking can be considered the equivalent to the national anthem. Being a patriotic people, everyone does it, seemingly every waking moment. Hawking stems from the smoky houses, which lead to horrible respiratory diseases. People must constantly, to put it as delicately as possible, "clear their throats." This consists of an ungodly noise that can be heard blocks away, starting deep in the chest and reaching a crescendo as a huge glob.... Well, let's save this for another time.

Trouble in Terontola

by William Petrocelli

FOR A TRAVELER, trouble spots are always personal. Those sucked into the Bermuda Triangle or crushed on the rocks between Scylla and Charybdis probably think such places are universally cursed, but the tens of thousands who come through those places unscathed wouldn't think so. For them there's probably some other, personal trouble spot—some place like Terontola. This nondescript railroad station between Rome and Florence means nothing to most people, but Terontola is my own personal black hole. In three chances it's gotten me every time.

One of Terontola's attacks came in the form of nausea. The Terontola train station was the launching point of a stomach-churning, mouth-holding, rail trip into Siena—one that culminated in an extravagant form of up-chucking that reverberated throughout the stone corridors of our Renaissance hotel like cheers from the *Palio.*

The next assault was sneakier. My wife, Elaine, and I contributed to our troubles by becoming entranced with a rather shy-looking woman who got on the train at the same time as we did in Perugia. She began telling us the story of her life in halting English, but as we got closer and closer to Terontola her English became clearer and clearer and her story racier and racier. At the last moment we broke free from her tale, looking out the window for the connecting train that was supposed to take us to Orvieto before it continued on to Rome. Our traveling companion pointed helpfully to the platform a couple of tracks away and to the sign that said *Roma*. We boarded, stashed our suitcases in one of the compartments, and stationed ourselves against the window on the right side to await the spectacular view of Orvieto high on its plateau that was due to unfold as we approached the city. Fields rolled by, and then a tunnel, and then more fields. The trip seemed to take longer than it should. Soon we were rolling through what appeared to be an Italian suburbia, wondering how this charming Umbrian town could have acquired such unattractive surroundings. A sign finally brought us to our senses: *Roma Ostiense*. Not only had our Rome-bound train not stopped in Orvieto, but it had somehow managed to erase it entirely from the trip. We learned later that the particular train we were on actually went by tunnel underneath Orvieto, denying us even a view of the city that we had planned to visit. Where was the Orvieto train? I'm still convinced that Terontola somehow gobbled it up.

But were it not for the third incident a decade ago, I'd be prepared to forgive Terontola for all of its transgressions. That day began hopefully as we prowled the markets of the Piazza *Santa Maria Novella* near the Florence train station, picking up the ingredients for an on-board picnic that we planned for the train ride to Assisi. A loaf of bread, a little salad, a chunk of *Parmigiana*—all nicely balanced by a slightly extravagant bottle of Chianti. The day was overcast, and it became almost misty as we rolled through the Tuscan countryside. We had to change trains to get to Assisi, and where would that change occur? Terontola, of course. As we pulled into the station, I grabbed the suitcases and Elaine scooped up the loose bags and hand baggage. She led the way down the aisle, and I followed. Then she reached the steps. In retrospect, it's hard to think of them as steps—they were more like a ladder at a ninety-degree angle to the ground with wet metal rungs.

Elaine took one step on to the first rung and then a second into space, plummeting towards the wet walkway.

Watching a disaster from above gives one a rare, god-like perspective. But unlike the deity, I was powerless to stop this one. As she hit the ground all activity around the train station stopped. People turned at the sound of her fall and then instinctively converged on the spot where she lay, many leaping across the tracks to come to her assistance (proving, I should point out, that the people of Terontola are wonderful even if the concept of Terontola is malevolent). I stumbled down the ladder in a daze, trying to avoid slipping myself. Below me I could see Elaine—lying still, face down, with her arms spread out. But that wasn't the worst of it: what sent me into shock was a red puddle oozing out from underneath her body.

As you may have guessed, this story ends in low farce rather than high tragedy. For days thereafter as we visited some particularly gloomy church, seeing portraits of saints in dramatically penitent postures, Elaine would display the bloody bruises on her hands and remind me that she too had the stigmata. In fact, even now when we approach a treacherous walkway that has the potential for us to make spectacular fools of ourselves, it's traditional for us to warn each other with a "Stiggie Alert."

But it wouldn't be right to end this with Elaine lying face down on the pavement in Terontola. She finally got up, although a bit slowly. We thanked profusely all the people who had rushed to her aid, particularly the man who had recovered her purse from where it had landed a couple of tracks away. None of her body parts were injured or broken; she was able to keep going.... But she had completely squashed a rather innocent bottle of Chianti.

Maui for One

by Roger Rapoport

AS AN EXPERIENCED business traveler, I knew the drill. Hug the wife, kiss the kids, and make a mad dash for the airport. Regular calls home to check up on the family, loving postcards, and, most important, presents for all.

But for the first time in more than twenty years of marriage, I wasn't coming home to a grand reunion at the front door. Shortly before I took off for Maui, my wife and I agreed to separate and file for divorce. Weeks after my return we did.

The last time I had traveled as a single person Richard Nixon was in the White House and gas was thirty-nine cents a gallon. But my friends, especially the married ones, said not to worry. Making new friends would be a breeze in the islands. Some even expressed a little envy at the possibilities—single and loving it on Maui.

I'm not sure how long after touch down in Kaanapali that I realized I was, in fact, the only single person on Maui that week. From the baggage carousel, to the rent-a-car desk, to the check-in line at my first hotel in Wailea, I was surrounded by couples. There were honeymooners stepping out of sightseeing helicopters, college kids embracing next to the rumbling ersatz volcano at the Grand Hyatt, and gay couples breakfasting next door at the heavenly Hotel Hana Maui.

Nowhere did the situation hit home faster than at restaurants where perplexed waiters grandly swept away the second table setting as soon as I took my seat. At the Westin's Swan Court, I was seated directly adjacent to a multigeneration family gathering of thirty toasting a couple's grand fiftieth anniversary.

To be honest, I can't tell you where Maui's singles were that week—perhaps they were all off attending a convention in Honolulu. The only thing I can say for sure is that when, by chance, I did actually run into someone who claimed to be unattached, they were about as accessible as rum punch at a Mormon wedding. On my first morning in Maui I boarded a snorkeling boat to Molokini where a divorced mom from Seattle asked if I would be interested in joining her group for a luau that evening. "I'll give you a call at your hotel and let you know where to meet us," she said as we disembarked that evening. My message light never blinked.

Another woman from Moscow interning for a short time at a Kaanapali hotel brightened during a guided tour when I mentioned that I knew about the Russian hospital where her father practiced. Unfortunately our agreed upon dinner date was canceled with a sweet note left in my box at the front desk. Perhaps, she suggested, we could get together with her fiancé on my next visit to Moscow.

As I scoured the island for bright new restaurants and charming condominiums, I found myself passing many of the landmarks visited before our nuclear family had split. I paused to gaze at crescent beaches where my kids had frolicked blissfully, the former site of Jesse's Luau where rain had canceled the festivities for the first time in six years, and, of course, the volcanic splendors of Haleakala. Trooping through Kapalua I flashed back to memories of my son and daughter, waterlogged, slightly sunburned, and lei clad.

Calls back home, a highlight of any trip, now had a different feel. One night there was an emergency message: my son, set to go out for a big evening, wondered if I could explain long distance how to tie a Windsor knot in one of my silk ties.

Prodded by demanding faxes from my insistent employer, I worked late into the evening to cover all the ground necessary to make sure that our new guide to Maui would be encyclopedic. But as I hustled to document hundreds of reasons why Maui was a great vacation destination, it became clear that I certainly didn't fit the tourist profile of this celebrated destination. In fact, if you have just separated, you would be better off in Las Vegas, Leningrad, Lhasa—anywhere but the honeymoon capital of the world.

When I returned home there was a letter waiting for me from a friend in Ireland.

"Meet any interesting women in Maui?" she asked. "Or is it too early for that?"

Unfolding the hide-a-bed in my home office that night, I thought about all the interesting couples I had met in Maui, people joined at the hip, reciting vows, promising to never stray, to remain faithful, and above all, to love, honor, and cherish one another. I thought about the wedding parties I had seen and the honeymoon suites I'd inspected in the line of duty.

All were beautiful places guaranteed to make love last. I had even photographed a few to show to the bosses back home. Alas, those pictures, along with the rest of my portfolio, never made the return trip. On my last night at the Grand Hyatt, I put my camera down outside my room while bringing in a box of notes. By the time I returned, my camera had disappeared. When I reported the theft, a matching pair of security officers arrived on the scene to take my report.

"Who else was with you when this happened?" asked guard number one.

"I'm here by myself."

"You can level with us," said guard number two with a knowing wink. "We won't tell your wife a thing."

Bad Things Don't Happen to Me

by Jan Morris

WHEN I WAS a foreign correspondent, long ago, it always piqued me that more exciting things happened to my colleagues than ever happened to me. They were arrested by secret policemen in Hungary. They were threatened by Congolan war-lords. Their dispatches led to diplomatic incidents, or got them invitations to stern Presidential *tête-à-têtes*. Not me. As I reported year after year from around the world, crime and calamity, Mafia and Minister, KGB and CIA alike took no notice of me at all.

Now that my travels are of a still more literary kind (for even when I was reporting a war or a political assassination, I always thought of myself as writing *belles-lettres*)—now that I am only a wandering essayist, I find that I am still immune to misadventure. The appalling events that have befallen my colleagues in this book never strike at me. Just once in a while I wish they would; but then again, what's so special about bad luck?

It is part of life's experience, that's all, and is really no more interesting, and no more useful to the writer, than the happy surprises of travel, like finding a decent pot of tea in Indianapolis, or seeing a Laurel and Hardy film (as long ago I did) in a particularly unprepossessing suburb of Baghdad. Like good news, easy travel does not often inspire literature, still less anthologies. It is generally good only for opportunist gush in travel magazines. Yet a happy progress can provide just as valuable grist for the literary mill as any disastrous mishap.

A Sudanese Minister of National Guidance once told me that my professional duty was to write "thrilling, attractive, and good news, coinciding where possible with the truth." I have taken his advice seriously. I don't know if there is a word for the gift of stumbling across nasty surprises, but I do know that serendipity, the gift of bumping into pleasant ones, is a most fortunate tool for the writer to possess. Nothing very awful occurred to Alexander Kinglake anywhere in *Eothen*, to my mind the supreme travel book, and Patrick Leigh Fermor, the greatest of our contemporaries in this field, seems usually to travel in a condition of charmed good fortune and self-amusement.

Not that the ability to attract good luck is really a gift (though Napoleon thought it was, at least in generals). I do think it likely, nevertheless, that if you expect the best you get the best. Being of sanguine temperament myself I have so far found in life, as in travel, that the worst seldom comes about. I never expected to be arrested, when I went prying into the secret prisons of Nasser's Egypt, or tried to cheat the Soviet censorship, and I never was; just as, contrary to many complaints in women's magazines, I always expect a good table when I am eating out alone, and nearly always get one.

I claim no merit for this. I still admire the capacity of friends and fellow-workers to get themselves into the most terrible fixes, the most daunting situations, and to turn them into literature. I would love to have been able to contribute to the body of this collection, instead of adding a quibble at the end. My point is only that the one tendency is as good as the other, when it comes to the writing art; just as the most ordinary activities of daily existence, going to a chiropodist, buying a newspaper, boarding a bus, talking to a housewife on a park bench, can contribute as much to a composition as any great set-piece of the traveling experience. Perhaps one really should stay home?

It does sometimes occur to me, though, that I may be deceiving myself. Is it simply that I am better at writing about the happy than the unhappy? Do I subconsciously put the misadventures out of my mind? Have I, too, been challenged in nightmare electric baths in Japan, accused of being improperly dressed in posh restaurants in Manhattan, massaged by tattooed giantesses of Belize, assaulted by Guatemalan ants or eyed by rats in Madagascar lavatories, and simply forgotten all about it?

Surely not. Nothing bad ever happens to me.

Afterword:
How This Book Was Written

by Roger Rapoport

WHEN ELAINE AND Bill Petrocelli and their colleagues Marguerita Castanera and Kathryn Barcos began the Book Passage Travel Writers' Conference in 1992, many friends wondered if it would work. Travel writers schedule their lives a year ahead. Travel publishers are always on a deadline and how on earth do you actually teach travel writing?

But the announcements had only been posted for a few days when the RSVPs started pouring in. Jan Morris agreed to fly in from England. Tony Wheeler promised to pop over from Australia. Editors at Fodor's, Moon, Birnbaum, Condé Nast Traveler, pros like Georgia Hesse (second from left on the cover), and Shirley Streshinsky signed on.

Thanks to a terrific response, the Book Passage crew decided to repeat the conference in 1993. The new announcement included other impressive names like Mary Morris and Eric Newby. But what caught my eye this time was a student essay writing contest called "My Favorite Worst Travel Experience." As an experienced travel writer, I could relate to that.

"I think there might be a book here," I told the Book Passage folks. They agreed and you are holding the proud result of our collaboration.

Contributors to this volume include world class novelists like Isabel Allende and Barbara Kingsolver. Prominent writers who have been hailed for their travel books and essays, such as Paul Theroux, Jan Morris, and Mary Morris are also represented. If you travel, chances are that you have used books by other authors like Tony Wheeler and Rick Steves.

Many veteran travel writers are represented in these pages including Stacy Ritz, Richard Harris, Joe Cummings, Donald George, and Christopher Baker. Each has provided an insiders look at the special joys of traveling for a living.

We are also pleased to introduce some exciting new talents discovered at Book Passage Travel Writers' Conference like Carole Peccorini, winner of the essay contest that inspired this volume, along with other students.

Most of the authors have agreed to donate their royalties to Oxfam America, the international relief organization, or another charity of their choice. The publisher is also making a contribution to Oxfam America.

A number of pieces deserve special mention. Mary Mackey's night of the ants and scorpions, Muriel Dobbin's odyssey with LBJ, and Jeff Greenwald's shocking account of water "torture" in Japan, provide three compelling reasons to remain near home and hearth. In each case the author came, saw, and, fortunately for us all, lived to recount the story.

My colleagues Deborah Dunn and Wendy Logsdon at RDR Books did a wonderful job of bringing this manuscript to completion. Each lent their talents to the final product, gently shaping and guiding each piece to publication.

Finally, I'd like to say a few words about the Book Passage gang. Kathryn Barcos, who co-administered the Travel Writers' Conference, assisted this project from beginning to end. My co-editor Marguerita Castanera approached this project with endless enthusiasm and her customary efficiency. Many of the best pieces in this book are the result of her courteous prodding.

Bill and Elaine Petrocelli, two booksellers who have made

a career of befriending authors and readers, have now become publishers with their very own imprint. To those of us who have benefited from their energy and enthusiasm, this step makes perfect sense. To them and all of you who have agreed to join us on this journey to that special place somewhere beyond the security zone of guided tours, I say happy trails and bon voyage.

About the Authors

Isabel Allende

Isabel Allende is the internationally acclaimed author of *The House of the Spirits, Eva Luna, Stories of Eva Luna, Of Love and Shadows,* and *The Infinite Plan.* Her books have won numerous awards, been translated into twenty-seven languages, and are best sellers in the United States, Europe, Latin America, and Australia. Recently, her novel, *The House of the Spirits,* was made into a movie starring Meryl Streep, Glenn Close, and Jeremy Irons.

Lisa Alpine

Lisa Alpine is Creative Director of *Travel Press International,* a contributing writer to *Common Ground, Specialty Travel Index,* and the *Pacific Sun,* and freelances to many other publications. When not in front of her typewriter pounding out another story, she is teaching expressive dance or is outside doing something adventurous be it whitewater kayak guiding, scuba diving in Egypt, volcano climbing in Indonesia, or horsepacking in the Sierra. Her eleven-year-old son, Galen, usually comes along and always has a good campfire story to contribute about many a misadventure.

Christopher Baker

Christopher Baker has been published in over 150 publications worldwide including *Newsweek,* the *Los Angeles Times,* and *Writer's Digest.* He has authored several books including the *Costa Rica Handbook* and the *Thomas Cook Guide to Jamaica.*

He has escorted tour groups to New Zealand, Hong Kong, Korea, and his homeland of England. Among other writing awards, Baker has won two Lowell Thomas Travel Journalism awards.

Richard Bangs

Richard Bangs has capsized boats on six continents. His latest book is *Peaks, Searching for High Ground Across the Continents* from Taylor Publishing. He is the author of eleven other books, including *Whitewater Adventure* and *Islandgods*. He lives on the Hayward Fault in Oakland, California.

Larry Collins

Larry Collins, a former correspondent for UPI and *Newsweek,* is the author of the bestselling novels *Fall From Grace* and *Maze*. His latest book, *Black Eagles*, will be published in the spring of 1995. He has also co-authored, with Dominique Lapierre, five international bestsellers: *The Fifth Horseman, Freedom at Midnight, Or I'll Dress you in Mourning, Oh Jerusalem,* and *Is Paris Burning?* He divides his time between France, England, and the United States.

Alev Lytle Croutier

Alev Lytle Croutier was born in Turkey. She has taught film courses, directed films, and written screenplays—among them *Tell Me A Riddle* based on Tillie Olsen's novel. She was the first person to be awarded a Guggenheim fellowship for screenplay writing. For seven years she was the executive editor of Mercury House publishing company. Her books include *Harem: The World Behind the Veil, Taking the Waters,* and the upcoming *Night Life*. Croutier lives in San Francisco.

Joe Cummings

Joe Cummings has written a number of acclaimed travel guides on Southeast Asia and North America for Lonely Planet Publications and Moon Publications. He has contributed articles to *Outside, The Independent, BBC Holidays,* the *San Francisco Examiner, The Asia Record, Geographical, World & I,* and *Earth Journal.*

Barbara Ann Curcio

Barbara Ann Curcio is a travel columnist for the *Washington Post,* where her travel features also appear regularly. She frequently writes about lifestyle and the arts.

Muriel Dobbin

Muriel Dobbin was born in Scotland and came to the United States thirty years ago. She worked for the *Baltimore Sun* for twenty-five years, as a White House correspondent in Washington and as West Coast Bureau Chief based in San Francisco. She is now a national correspondent and White House reporter for the Washington Bureau of McClatchy Newspapers. She has written four books including *A Taste for Power,* which is about a vampire running for President.

Michael Dorris

Michael Dorris is the author of the novel *A Yellow Raft in Blue Water* and *Working Men,* short stories, as well as two novels for young readers, *Morning Girl* and *Guests.* His non-fiction includes a collection of essays, *Paper Trail,* and *The Broken Cord,* which won the National Book Critics Circle award in 1989.

Susan Dunlap

Mystery novelist Susan Dunlap is known for her popular Berkeley series featuring homicide detective, Jill Smith, in *Time Expired* and *Death and Taxes*. Her mystery creations also include PG&E meter reader Vejay Haskell in *The Last Annual Slugfest*, and former forensic pathologist turned private eye Kiernan O'Shaughnessy in her latest book *High Fall.*

Janet Fullwood

Janet Fullwood spent lots of time on the "Gringo Trail" through Latin America in the 1970s. A six-year stint as travel editor of the *Dallas Times Herald* took her to more than forty countries in the 1980s. She now lives in California, where she is Travel Editor of the *Sacramento Bee.*

Donald George

Donald George roams the globe, in fancy and in fact, as the Travel Editor of the *San Francisco Examiner.* His writings have won awards and have appeared in many places. He is chairman of the annual Book Passage Travel Writers' Conference.

Molly Giles

Molly Giles, author of *Rough Translations,* teaches creative writing at San Francisco State University and the University of Hawaii, and occasionally leads writing workshops at Book Passage. She has finished a second collection of stories, *Talking To Strangers,* and is working on a novel.

Joe Gores

Joe Gores is the author of ten novels including the Edgar-nominated *32 Cadillacs* and *Come Morning,* as well as numerous

screenplays and teleplays. He has received the Edgar Allen Poe award in three categories for his work: Best First Novel, Best Short Story, and Best TV Series Segment. Gores has based many of his novels on his twelve years experience as a San Francisco private detective.

Judith Greber

Judith Greber is the author of four novels, *Easy Answers, The Silent Partner, Mendocino,* and *As Good As It Gets.* Under the name of Gillian Roberts, she writes mystery novels featuring Philadelphia English teacher Amanda Pepper. These titles include *How I Spent My Summer Vacation, Caught Dead in Philadelphia, Philly Stakes, I'd Rather be in Philadelphia,* and *With Friends Like These.*

Scott Christopher Green

A New York City native, Scott Christopher Green now lives and works as a freelance writer in Emeryville, California.

Jeff Greenwald

Jeff Greenwald's work has appeared in the *Washington Post, San Francisco Examiner, Mother Jones,* and *Los Angeles Times.* He is the author of *Mister Raja's Neighborhood* and *Shopping for Buddhas.* He is currently traveling around the world collecting research for a new book. He sends dispatches from abroad on Internet via Global Network Navigator.

Helen Gurley Brown

Author of the bestselling *Sex And The Single Girl* (1962), Helen has since written six books including *The Late Show, a Semi-wild but Practical Survival Plan for Women Over 50.* In 1965, Helen became Editor-In-Chief of *Cosmopolitan* magazine.

Married to award-winning producer, David Brown, Helen says she is "a health nut, a feminist, an irredeemable but contented workaholic, and passionately interested in the relationship between men and women."

Eric Hansen

Eric Hansen, author of the acclaimed *Stranger in the Forest, Motoring with Mohammed,* and *The Traveler,* was born in San Francisco, and has traveled extensively throughout the Middle East and Asia over the past twenty years.

He has worked as a barber in Mother Teresa's Home for the Dying Destitute in Calcutta, and, in 1987, he was shipwrecked for two weeks on an uninhabited desert island in the Red Sea. In 1982 he spent five months traveling through the Borneo rain forest with the Penan, one of the last groups of nomadic hunters and gatherers on earth. *Stranger in the Forest* is the story of that journey.

In 1992 Hansen returned to Borneo to establish The Penan Guide Project, a guide service and literacy program which provides rural employment for the Penan by taking small groups of western visitors into the rain forest. Enquiries and donations can be sent to The Penan Guide Project, 918 9th Avenue, Sacramento, CA 95818.

Richard Harris

Richard Harris is the author of numerous guidebooks including *2 to 22 Days in the American Southwest, The New Key to Cancun and the Yucata,* and co-author of *The Maya Route.* A veteran travel guide editor, he practiced law in Colorado before turning to writing. Harris lives in Santa Fe.

Georgia Hesse

For twenty years Georgia Hesse was the Travel Editor at the *San Francisco Examiner*. Her byline appears in many national travel magazines including *Diversion Magazine, Condé Nast Traveler, Endless Vacation*, the *Chicago Tribune*, and *Newsday*. She has written and edited several guidebooks to France and Northern California.

Robert Holmes

Robert Holmes is an award-winning British photographer, and the first person to receive the Travel Photographer of the Year award from the Society of Magazine Photographers (in 1990 and 1992). His clients include *National Geographic, Life*, and *Travel & Leisure*. His fifteen books include destinations such as Hawaii, Baja, and San Francisco.

Pico Iyer

Pico Iyer is an essayist for *Time*, a Contributing Editor to *Condé Nast Traveler*, and the author of *Video Night in Kathmandu, The Lady and the Monk, Falling Off the Map*, and a forthcoming novel set in Cuba. He resides in Santa Barbara, California.

Louis B. Jones

Louis B. Jones is the author of the novels *Ordinary Money* and *Particles and Luck*. He lives in Mill Valley, California.

Alice Kahn

Alice Kahn has been called a teacher, a nurse, a nurse-practitioner, a newspaper columnist, a humorist, a writer, and much worse. Her books include *Multiple Sarcasm* and *Fun with Dirk and Bree* as well as short stories.

Evelyn Kieran

Evelyn Kieran served as Travel Editor of the *San Diego Tribune* for fifteen years. She has traveled the globe many times but mostly with nothing but great memories. She currently writes a column called "Travel Solo" in *Travel 50 & Beyond*. She resides in San Francisco.

Barbara Kingsolver

Barbara Kingsolver is a fiction writer, mother, environmentalist, and human rights activist who grew up in rural Kentucky and now lives in Tucson, Arizona. Her six books have received numerous awards, including the *Los Angeles Times'* fiction prize, and four successive nominations for the American Booksellers Book of the Year award. She still doesn't do pumps.

Dominique Lapierre

Author, journalist, and philanthropist, Dominique Lapierre has written, with Larry Collins, *Is Paris Burning?*, ... *Or I'll Dress You in the Mourning*, *O Jerusalem*, *Freedom at Midnight*, and *The Fifth Horseman*.

In 1981 Lapierre met Mother Teresa, who took him into some of the slums of Calcutta where she was working. This experience changed Lapierre's life. After two years of research, he published *The City of Joy*, an epic story about man's capacity to survive the worst adversities. The book received many awards and was made into a major motion picture. With the royalties of *The City of Joy* and donations from his readers, Lapierre has been supporting a network of humanitarian actions in Calcutta and the Ganges delta.

Lapierre's association for managing this action now has a United States representative for these charities—ACTION

AID USA, c/o Marie B. Allizon, 7419 Lisle Avenue, Falls Church, VA 22043—to which readers can send their donations.

Suzanne Lipsett

Northern California novelist and essayist Suzanne Lipsett is also an independent editor who has worked with authors and publishers as a "midwife of books" for twenty-five years. Her most recent titles are *Remember Me*, a portrait of a family in stories, and *Surviving a Writer's Life*, a series of essays on writing, memory, and imagination.

Mary Mackey

Mary Mackey is the author of *The Year the Horses Came*, several volumes of poetry, and freelance articles which have been published in *The Saturday Evening Post, Holiday, The New American Review*, and others. She has also written film scripts including the award winning screenplay *Silence* directed by John Korty in 1974. Mary is presently a professor of English and writer in residence at California State University Sacramento where she teaches creative writing and film.

Naomi Mann

Naomi Mann, a freelance writer based in San Francisco, is the author of *Forms of the Essay: The American Experience*. Her story is adapted from *Dear Mom/Dear Jessica: Journey to Bliss*, a work-in-progress about mothers and daughters, travels in India, gurus, saints, and other related wonders, marvels, and hazardous enterprises. Her daughter, Jessica Rattner, is coauthor of the book. Mann was a runner up in the 1993 Book Passage Travel Writers' Conference award.

Adrianne Marcus

Adrianne Marcus is a full time writer of poetry, journalism, and fiction. She has been published in various magazines including *Parade, Travel & Leisure, Atlantic Monthly,* and *Cosmopolitan.* Marcus has just completed her first novel, titled *Chefs,* and is currently at work on a new book, based on Celtic legend, "The Morrigan's Crow." She lives in San Rafael, California with her husband, Ian Wilson, her wolf-dog, Lady MacBeth, a border collie mix, Charlie, plus a terrorist cat, Hecate.

Claudia J. Martin

Claudia J. Martin lives in the San Francisco Bay Area with her dog, Tralfaz, and devotes as much time as possible to traveling, writing, photography, and occasionally being a pastry chef. Her travel stories have appeared in the *San Francisco Examiner.*

Jan Morris

Jan Morris is a Welsh writer of history, autobiography, and fiction as well as of travel essays. Her next book will be an affectionate study of Admiral Lord "Jacky" Fisher (1841–1920), of the British Royal Navy, with whom she plans to have an affair in the afterlife. Her many acclaimed books include *Destinations, Great Port, Sydney, Hong Kong, Locations,* and *Venetian Empire.*

Mary Morris

Mary Morris is the author of seven books, including *Nothing to Declare: Memoirs of a Woman Traveling Alone* and *Wall-to-Wall: From Beijing to Berlin by Rail.* Her novels include *A Mother's Love.* She lives in Brooklyn, New York, with her husband Larry O'Connor and their daughter.

Marcia Muller and Bill Pronzini

Marcia Muller has authored twenty-one mystery novels, fourteen of them in the Sharon McCone series, and contributed numerous short stories, articles, and reviews to national publications. With Bill Pronzini, she co-edited ten anthologies, as well as *1001 Midnights: The Aficionado's Guide to Mystery and Detective Fiction.* In 1993, the Private Eye Writers of America presented her with their Life Achievement Award for her contribution to the genre. McCone's fifteenth case, *Till the Butchers Cut Him Down,* was published in July, 1994.

A full-time professional writer since 1969, Bill Pronzini has published (alone and in collaboration with others) more than forty novels, including twenty-one in his popular "Nameless Detective" series; three non-fiction books; six collections of short stories; and numerous uncollected stories, articles, essays, and book reviews. He has also edited upwards of eighty anthologies. His most recent novels are *Demons* and *With an Extreme Burning.* He has received two Shamus awards and the Lifetime Achievement Award from the Private Eye Writers of America, and five nominations for the Mystery Writers of America Edgar award.

Katherine Neville

Katherine Neville is the author of *The Eight,* an adventure novel filled with "history, mystery, and magic," which was inspired by her experience working for OPEC in North Africa. *A Calculated Risk,* a *New York Times* "notable book" is an international financial intrigue based upon her experiences on Wall Street and as an executive of Bank of America in San Francisco. Her books are in print in seventeen languages.

Larry O'Connor

Larry O'Connor is a journalist and editor. He is co-editor of *Maiden Voyages* and is author of a memoir, *The Tip of the Iceberg*. His articles have appeared in the *New York Times,* the *Globe and Mail, New Woman* magazine, and *Travel Holiday.* He is editor of the *Chelsea Clinton News* in New York City.

Carole L. Peccorini

Carole Peccorini knew she could be at home anywhere as she sweltered in equatorial Borneo while Millie, an adolescent female orangutan, diligently licked her left leg for the better part of an hour. She presently travels and writes with women in Italy and Greece, and one of her paintings was on the book cover of Anne Hillman's *The Dancing Animal Woman.* Peccorini was the winner of the 1993 Book Passage Travel Writers' Conference award.

William Petrocelli

William Petrocelli is the author of *Low Profile: How to Avoid the Privacy Invaders* and co-author of *Sexual Harassment on the Job: What it is and How to Stop It.* He and his wife, Elaine, are the co-owners of Book Passage in Corte Madera, California.Petrocelli lives in Mill Valley, California.

Roger Rapoport

Publisher of RDR Books, Roger Rapoport is the author of numerous books including *Into The Sunlight: Life After the Iron Curtain, Great Cities of Eastern Europe,* and the 2 to 22 day guides to California and the Rockies. He co-authored the 2 to 22 day guides to Asia and Around The World with Burl Willes.

Stacy Ritz

Stacy Ritz is the author and co-author of six travel books, including the award-winning *The New Key to Belize*. A former staff writer for the *Tampa Tribune* and adjunct professor of journalism at Florida International University, she is a regular contributor to the *Miami Herald* and the *Fort Lauderdale Sun-Sentinel*. She has written for the *Washington Post, Detroit News, Caribbean Travel & Life*, and other publications. She is currently writing a travel guide to the Carolinas.

Stan Sesser

Stan Sesser, the author of *The Lands of Charm and Cruelty*, writes frequently on Asia for the *New Yorker*. He has also reported for the *Wall Street Journal* and taught at the Graduate School of Journalism at the University of California at Berkeley, the city where he lives.

Rick Steves

Seattle-ite Rick Steves has spent twenty-two summers exploring Europe. He has written twelve guidebooks including the popular *Europe Through the Back Door*, a series of country guides, art guides, and phrasebooks. He hosts and writes the national PBS TV series "Travels in Europe with Rick Steves," publishes a free quarterly Europe through the Back Door newsletter, and is learning more and more about travel with children.

Shirley Streshinsky

Shirley Streshinsky, a Berkeley resident, is the author of novels including *The Shores of Paradise, Gifts of the Golden Mountain, A Time Between,* and the biography, *Audubon: Life and*

Art in the American Wilderness. She is also a freelance writer whose work has been published in *Travel & Leisure, Condé Nast Traveler, Glamour, Redbook,* and the *San Francisco Examiner.* Shirley and Suna will be traveling together to Singapore for more adventures.

Paul Theroux

Paul Theroux's novels and travel literature span the globe. His novels include *Millroy the Magician, The Mosquito Coast, Saint Jack,* and *My Secret History.* Among his distinguished travel books are *The Great Railway Bazaar, The Old Patagonian Express,* and *The Happy Isles of Oceania.* He lives in Honolulu.

Linda Watanabe McFerrin

Linda Watanabe McFerrin's travel stories have appeared in the *San Francisco Examiner,* the *Washington Post,* and other publications. She is the author of two poetry collections: *Chisel, Rice Paper, Stone,* and *The Impossibility of Redemption is Something We Hadn't Figured On,* and is currently at work on a novel set in Japan. She was winner of the 1992 Book Passage Travel Writers' Conference award.

Tony Wheeler

Tony Wheeler was born in England but spent most of his youth overseas. He returned to England to do a university degree in engineering, but then dropped out on the Asian overland trail with his wife, Maureen. They've been traveling, writing, and publishing guidebooks ever since, having set up Lonely Planet Publications in the mid-'70s. Travel for the Wheelers is now considerably enlivened by their daughter Tashi and son Kieran.

Burl Willes

Burl Willes learned to print his name and address at age four so he could get a travel brochure in the mail. Since then he has used every excuse to travel "off the beaten path." He started Trips Out Travel in 1970, wrote a travel column for the RDR Syndicate, and travel books for John Muir Publications.

Abigail Wine

Abigail Wine lives in Oakland, California. A bilingual educator and special education advocate, she always felt that living in the Bay Area, with its diverse communities, prepared her for travel abroad. She continues to support the revolutionary aspirations of Cuban youth, and opposes the United States trade embargo.

Oxfam America

MOST OF THE contributors to this book are donating their royalties to Oxfam America, a nonprofit international agency funding self-help development and disaster relief projects in Africa, Asia, the Americas, and the Caribbean.

Oxfam's grants support local groups in twenty-eight countries including the United States, working to increase food production and economic self-reliance. Oxfam America is one of eight autonomous Oxfams around the world. The international family of Oxfams has earned a global reputation for innovative yet realistic aid to some of the most resource-poor people in the world.

Oxfam focuses on small-scale projects averaging $24,000 where a few dollars go a long way, projects that set an example and create changes reaching beyond the project itself. Oxfam project partners are establishing fish hatcheries in Cambodia, providing nonformal education to primary school children, especially girls in India, and fostering the growth of indigenous leaders in Ecuador. In Ethiopia, Oxfam partners have introduced an improved plow that doubles crop yields, while Oxfam's projects in El Salvador are helping to build a new society after twelve years of civil strife. A program in Dominica helps diversify agriculture and supports the development of local markets while a Bangladesh project makes it possible for women heads of households to increase their income.

Through offices in Boston, Washington, and San Francisco, Oxfam America has also created an extensive educational program in the United States, focusing on ways to alleviate hunger and poverty and creating an awareness about the root causes of hunger.

The publishers of this book encourage readers to support Oxfam America's work around the world. For information on how to join and support this organization please call or write to Oxfam America, 26 West Street, Boston, Massachusetts, 02111-1206; 1-800-OXFAM US.